BELONGS TO:

_____

TAROT CARDS

AS A DIVINATION TOOL

Tarot cards have been used as a divination tool since the early sixteenth century starting in the country of _____. They were developed as a tool to demonstrate the various _____ of life as in the Major Arcana, and then also as a way to explain the various stages of each of the four major _____ people encounter in life such as thoughts and ideas (Swords), emotions (Cups), passion and purpose (Wands) and material possessions (Pentacles).

The tarot card deck is meant to walk an individual through the _____ of a cycle to the completion of a cycle, only to start again when the next occasion arises. There are many _____ and meanings involved with each card that can leave an inexperienced reader confused. It takes time and _____ to understand the entire deck, but it is possible to master it with enough study and learning to use your intuition. There are many ways to learn to read. You must find the way that works for you.

The tarot deck can be used to receive messages from your _____ as well as from your guides. They use the deck to convey messages to the reader. It is only _____ of the ways for guides to relay messages, but it is an easy way for guides if the reader understands how to interpret the message. They may answer a certain question from the reader, or they may simply relay a needed message. _____ card spreads are used to relay extended messages over many cards.

TAROT CARDS

AS A DIVINATION TOOL

The message is meant for that particular _____ in time, based on the circumstances at that same moment in time. Because every human has _____, the message can change at any time - because something has changed with the person the message is meant for. The message is strictly meant for that moment.

Contrary to movies or television, tarot cards are not working with the dark arts but are instead working with _____ .The cards cannot predict the _____ and they cannot give any insight into the past reasoning for certain actions. They are a fun way to connect to Spirit and are sure to come in a _____ that interests you!

WORD BANK

Fill in the blanks with the following words:

- PATIENCE
- ITALY
- FREE WILL
- CYCLES
- EMOTIONS
- MULTIPLE
- FUTURE
- ONE
- HIGHER SELF
- MOMENT
- THEME
- SYMBOLS
- SPIRIT
- BEGINNING

TAROT TILES

REBUILD THE SENTENCE OR PHRASE

__ch T_r_t r__d_ng _s _n_q__ t_ ___ _t th_t m_m_nt _nd t_m_ b_c__s_ th_ c_rds w_rk w_th ___r _n_rg_ wh_ch _s ch_nn_l_d _nt_ th_ c_rds _nd ___ _r_ dr_wn t_ th_ c_rds th_t _r_ m_st r_l_v_nt t_ ___.

HINT: READINGS

_____

_____

_____

_____

_____

_____

_____

MISSING VOWELS

Can you rebuild the phrase? Fill in the missing vowels to complete the phrase.

FIND THE DIFFERENCE

CAN YOU FIND THE DIFFERENCES
BETWEEN THESE TWO IMAGES?

THERE ARE 18 DIFFERENCES

TAROT TILES

REBUILD THE SENTENCE OR PHRASE

Th_ M_j_r _rc_n_ T_r_t c_rds r_pr_s_nt th_ l_f_
l_ss_ns, k_rm_c _nfl__nc_s _nd th_ b_g
_rch_t_p_l th_m_s th_t _r_ _nfl__nc_ng ___r l_f_
_nd ___r s__l's j__rn__ t_ _nl_ght_nm_nt.

HINT: MAJOR ARCANA

_____

_____

_____

_____

_____

_____

_____

_____

_____

MISSING VOWELS

Can you rebuild the phrase? Fill in the missing vowels to complete the phrase.

HIDDEN OBJECT

CAN YOU FIND THE CUP IN THE PICTURE?

MAJOR ARCANA

THE FOOL'S JOURNEY

The Major Arcana comprises 22 cards that represent significant life events, also known as the "Fool's Journey". Each card stands for a stage of the journey - an *experience* that a person must incorporate to realize his wholeness.

The Fool stands for each of us as we begin our journey of life. He is a fool because only a *simple* soul has the *innocent* faith to undertake such a journey with all its hazards and pain. We will each find ourselves at every stage at some point in our lives. This journey is a tale of *expansion* and contraction that allows us to understand our stage on our own journey, or where we'll be arriving in the near future.

THE FOOL NEEDS TOOLS AND RESOURCES FOR THE JOURNEY. HE IS READY AND WILLING TO MEET POWERS, INFLUENCERS AND ADVISORS TO GUIDE THEM THROUGH

EMPOWERMENT · TRANSFORMATION · ENLIGHTENMENT

MAJOR ARCANA

THE FOOL'S JOURNEY

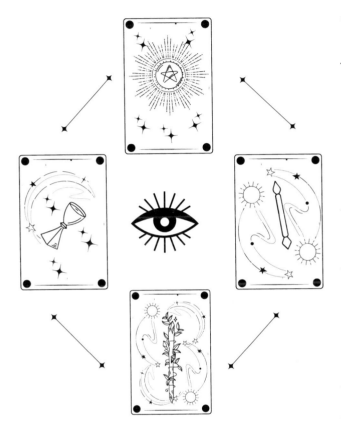

The journey is a metaphor for the journey through life and the phases and *trials* everyone will face. It's a chronological structure to represent important stages, lessons that have a profound impact on us, and junctures that have the potential to completely *change* our path. The journey is a *representation* of a myriad of possible journeys: people who are leaving home for the first time in his/her life, starting a new job, moving, graduating, a spiritual journey, and so on.

As you'll see, the Fool's Journey is not so foolish. Through perseverance and honesty he reestablishes the spontaneous courage that first drove his search, and now he is fully aware of his place in the *world*. In the end, his cycle is over, but the Fool will never stop growing. Soon he will be ready to *begin* a new journey that will lead him to ever greater levels of understanding.

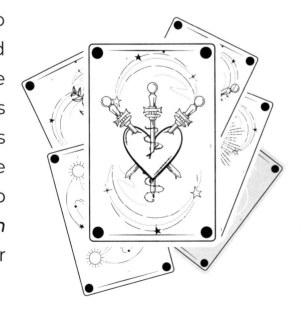

THE FOOL

- 0 -

A card of beginnings. At the start of his trip, the Fool is a newborn - fresh, open, and spontaneous. His arms are flung wide, and his head held high. He is ready to embrace whatever comes his way, but he is also oblivious to the cliff edge he is about to cross. The Fool is unaware of the hardships he will face as he ventures out to learn the lessons of the world.

The Fool reminds us to recognize the path of personal development within ourselves, and the stage upon that path where we find ourselves, in order to energize our movement toward deeper self-realization.

QUICK! JOT DOWN YOUR FIRST THOUGHTS ON THIS CARD.

O

THE FOOL.

THE FOOL

- 0 -

The time is now. Trust where the universe is taking you. Have an open and curious mind. Take the leap of faith even if you are unsure where you are going or if you are prepared. This is the time for potential and opportunity. Embrace the same carefree spirit as the Fool.

LOCATE THE FOLLOWING WORDS IN THE WORDSEARCH ON THE NEXT PAGE:

- ADVENTURE
- APPARENT FOLLY
- BLIND FAITH
- BOLDNESS
- CAREFREE
- CURIOSITY
- EXCITEMENT
- FAITH
- FOOLISHNESS
- INNOCENCE
- JOURNEY
- NEW BEGINNINGS
- SENSE OF WONDER
- SPONTANEITY
- OPTIMISM

THE FOOL

- 0 -

```
C C M P Q L A D U V K L X K M A V S J Q
B B R W O N Z M F P U P W S P O S B X O
C U G Q A O U G T Q D D X P E I C F X N
T N E M E T I C X E V V A T W N R W R E
B R Q A T W R B S F D R Z R O X Y S E W
Q W V W M N O D L E E H J E K V T I D B
V T E Q E Z H I F N H A T C M N I A N E
E B P D V U T T X D J C I V S E S O G
R V L H U J L F O P G Q R T A P N F W I
W K U I V T O C O E I W U G E F A A F N
S L E K R L N U Z P E P Z Q S D T E O N
X T U I L L Z E R J T M M K Q S N E E I
J K Q Y V S F N V N Z I F G R P O S S N
J E U U O B X T X D E L M E S S P S N G
I N N O C E N C E E A Y O I R B S E E S
E L T P G A E J A I D K W U S A W N S P
U N M O S I T W H W O A G D R M C D U N
K H N W U M H T I A F D N I L B G L L Z
W J S S E N H S I L O O F K O K N O S M
Y T I S O I R U C U F G F H V A O B P W
```

FINISH THE PICTURE

DESIGN YOUR OWN

MANY DECKS CARRY A THEME: ANIMALS, FAIRIES, WITCHES, POP CULTURE AND MORE. WHAT WOULD YOUR IDEAL THEME BE? DRAW THE FOOL CARD IN YOUR FAVORITE THEME.

THE MAGICIAN

-1-

EMPOWERMENT

On setting out, the Fool immediately encounters the Magician, one of the great balancing forces that make up the perceived world. The Magician is the guardian of the conscious mind and the tangible world.

The Magician represents the active, masculine power of creative impulse. He is also our conscious awareness. The Magician is the force that allows us to impact the world through a concentration of individual will and power.

He reveals to the Fool potentials and possibilities. Before him lays a map and the four elements. He acts as the Fools initiator and will accompany him unseen along his way as a spiritual master.

★ ★ ★

QUICK! JOT DOWN YOUR FIRST THOUGHTS ON THIS CARD.

THE MAGICIAN.

THE MAGICIAN

- 1 -

The Magician card means that you have the sheer willpower and desire to do anything you set your mind to. You have an innate power to create the inner world, in which your outer world will follow. You will not hesitate to tap into your full potential and become the best version of yourself. Move forward on an idea you have. You have the skills and knowledge to practice alchemy and become a master manifester. Commitment and planning are important.

LOCATE THE FOLLOWING WORDS IN THE WORDSEARCH ON THE NEXT PAGE:

- ACTION
- ADAPTATION
- COMMITMENT
- CRAFT
- CUNNING
- CONSCIOUS AWARENESS
- CONCENTRATION
- DOING
- FOCUS
- INSPIRED ACTION
- MANIFESTATION
- MASTERY
- RESOURCEFULNESS
- POWER
- SKILL

THE MAGICIAN

-1-

```
G  G  M  M  A  S  T  E  R  Y  S  P  B  L  T  A  B  M  J  X
L  R  R  Q  T  K  I  C  T  I  E  G  J  K  D  O  N  W  S  J
O  U  S  M  V  X  U  G  T  E  T  L  E  A  K  K  A  P  A  I
R  R  S  T  D  T  A  W  C  B  P  E  P  L  G  D  L  S  N  P
I  E  E  N  K  H  W  S  G  G  T  F  O  C  U  S  S  O  A
H  S  N  O  K  P  J  E  C  C  A  B  F  S  W  E  P  W  N  V
V  O  E  I  G  I  U  B  E  T  C  L  V  Q  G  I  E  E  I  K
A  U  R  T  O  N  G  F  I  Z  C  R  R  R  R  R  C  N  H  P
B  R  A  A  M  U  I  O  P  X  H  X  A  E  O  A  G  O  E  K
U  C  W  T  S  N  N  O  K  H  P  Z  D  F  C  L  H  I  J  N
I  E  A  S  Z  L  O  M  D  B  F  A  P  S  T  L  C  T  V  S
S  F  S  E  S  V  M  I  Q  T  C  O  P  P  Z  I  S  A  T  P
O  U  U  F  Q  D  C  W  T  T  Q  I  U  Z  C  K  J  R  I  I
V  L  O  I  V  G  L  S  I  C  F  Q  D  S  O  S  F  T  O  I
Z  N  I  D  C  Q  O  G  M  A  P  M  J  S  T  B  N  C  H
W  E  C  A  K  T  N  O  R  V  B  G  U  T  Q  R  Q  E  S  K
G  S  S  M  A  N  T  L  T  W  X  S  C  T  H  I  A  C  T  B
A  S  N  V  I  D  T  N  E  M  T  I  M  M  O  C  Z  N  Z  R
J  C  O  Q  X  B  V  U  W  Z  K  C  B  I  J  G  T  O  C  Q
T  R  C  Z  E  F  C  U  N  N  I  N  G  R  Q  W  E  C  Z  L
```

HIGH PRIESTESS

- 2 -
EMPOWERMENT

Next, the Fool encounters the High Priestess, the balancing force of the Magician. The High Priestess is the guardian of the subconscious mind and the teacher of sacred knowledge and hidden mysteries and represents the Fool's mother.

She tells the Fool to pay attention to their intuition and to trust their instincts. She advises him to trust himself before moving on and also to pay attention to his dreams.

The High Priestess is the mysterious unconscious. She provides the fertile ground in which creative events occur. The High Priestess is the unrealized potential waiting for an active principle to bring it to expression.

★ ★ ★

QUICK! JOT DOWN YOUR FIRST THOUGHTS ON THIS CARD.

THE HIGH PRIESTESS.

HIGH PRIESTESS

- 2 -

The High Priestess card means that you are to expand your inner knowledge. Reflect and learn about yourself through religion, nature, meditation, prayer, and spirituality. Connect to your intuition and access your inner wisdom over your conscious mind. If your insight is already heightened, the High Priestess asks you to trust that you are on the right path. Listen to your heart because it won't lead you astray.

LOCATE THE FOLLOWING WORDS IN THE WORDSEARCH ON THE NEXT PAGE:

- AUTHENTICITY
- CALM
- DIVINE FEMININE
- ENLIGHTENED
- INNER ILLUMINATION
- INTUITION
- KNOWING
- MYSTERY
- NON ACTION
- PATIENCE
- POTENTIAL
- PROPHECY
- SUBCONSCIOUS MIND
- UNCONSCIOUS AWARENESS
- WISDOM

HIGH PRIESTESS

- 2 -

```
D D R T R X A D Q R X I M O D S I W S N
A M I W C N A W Q D J K J L C O C V S O
I A F V E N L I G H T E N E D G E J E I
D D S E I X N C D Q C F N T B J C B N T
N Z K W W N H E H P E O V G M J N T E I
I R U N L I E X V I R H Q I V E E K R U
M H Z A N A N F A O A O T H N N I M A T
S P O C O G I Z E B B K P M P K T Z W N
U C I T I J K T W M J J R H V L A T A I
O D D T T Z B S N O I R B L E E P L S S
I P A Q C O T A O E S N A M F C N S U T
C Z H F A W X M Q E T B I A L N Y L O L
S K N D N J M W F F P O J N K A F T I G
N Z X M O G S M G P V L P L E D C D C T
O Z B Q N E V F P W Q N K V E K B H S L
C J P Z A H J N I R D E Q T G L F X N V
B N O I T A N I M U L L I R E N N I O V
U T X P K P B R J S V W R B S G S Q C K
S W A U T H E N T I C I T Y Q L S Z N P
P M Y S T E R Y H O K N O W I N G F U S
```

THE EMPRESS

- 3 -
EMPOWERMENT

The Empress represents the Fools earthly mother and from her he learns the female aspect of guidance. She appears when he needs nurturing. As he grows, the Fool becomes more and more aware of his surroundings as she reminds him to be aware of his emotions and to care for himself and others. The Empress teaches the Fool about nature and its cycles, nurturing and receptiveness.

The Empress represents the world of nature and sensation. A baby delights in exploring everything he touches, tastes, and smells. He cannot get enough of the sights and sounds that enchant his senses. It is natural to delight in the abundant goodness of Mother Earth who surrounds us with her support.

★ ★ ★

QUICK! JOT DOWN YOUR FIRST THOUGHTS ON THIS CARD.

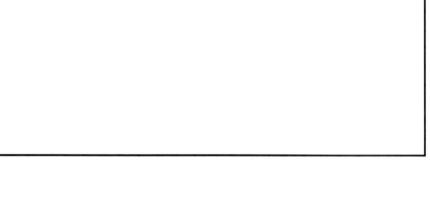

THE EMPRESS.

THE EMPRESS

When you have the Empress tarot card for your reading, it means that you're connected to your womanhood. You're fertile in many respects, and you have the drive to nurture. The biggest thing that The Empress wants you to do is to take care of yourself. The Empress also signifies abundance. Take time for gratitude for all that you have and that which surrounds you. Connect with nature, experience pleasure, nurture and care for others from a place of loving compassion and support.

LOCATE THE FOLLOWING WORDS IN THE WORDSEARCH ON THE NEXT PAGE:

- ABUNDANCE
- BEAUTY
- CREATIVE EXPRESSION
- ELEGANCE
- FEMININITY
- FERTILITY
- FLIRTING
- LOVING
- LUXURY
- MOTHERHOOD
- NATURE
- NURTURING
- SELFISHNESS
- SENSES
- SENSUALITY

THE EMPRESS

-3-

```
S C B L N P K Z D O L T K L X J M T A H
Q J U Q O I P A G I G U V G M J T S B N
I X V I H Q O W E L H Z X A P E O N A S
D O O H R E H T O M A P T U T S W O S E
F J N U J H R T V Q U J F A R P R I E N
I P R A Q F B N D D T Z C S O Y S S S S
B M E E M E S G N I R U T R U N P S N U
A Q O C A T F Y A O E D F P S A U E E A
P L I U N S O L T S W C H B T R R R S L
R T T L P A E S I I I N N X J K F P E I
N Y F U O T D L M R Z S N W I R X R T
E K K E A U H N F Z T I F X H K R E Q Y
P C L W R T C X U I O I N C U H R E S U
B G N V J T E F E B S Z N I I H L V F Z
V W I A B X I S X R A H K G M B X I C F
G B Q C G V L L J Q U I N X R E A T B V
O W N O M E T I I R E T T E W G F A O I
Z F D R T D L H F T L N A W S D F E K Q
N U J T B M K E D W Y E E N E S O R S P
S G N G N I V O L N W Z E W G P K C B V
```

THE EMPEROR

The next person the Fool encounters is his earthly father figure also known as the Emperor. He compliments the Empress with practical wisdom. He represents structure and authority and teaches about the material side of life providing guidelines on moral and ethical behavior. As a baby leaves his mother's arms, he learns that there are patterns in his world.

The Fool also encounters rules. He learns that his will is not always paramount and there are certain behaviors necessary for his well-being. There are people in authority who will enforce such guidelines. These restrictions can be frustrating, but, through the patient direction of the Father, the Fool begins to understand their purpose.

Together, the Emperor & Empress represent two parents for the Fool. They show that a balance is needed for his growth

★ ★ ★

QUICK! JOT DOWN YOUR FIRST THOUGHTS ON THIS CARD.

THE EMPEROR.

THE EMPEROR

EMPOWERMENT

The Emperor is the symbol of masculinity, which brings structure, rules, and systems into existence to bring about inner knowledge. This card suggests a need to find some sort of control, organization, and authority in your life. Pursue your goals strategically and methodically. Adopt the role of providing, protecting, and defending with stability and security. In return, you will earn loyalty and respect.

LOCATE THE FOLLOWING WORDS IN THE WORDSEARCH ON THE NEXT PAGE:

- AMBITION
- AUTHORITY
- DIRECTING
- ESTABLISHMENT
- FATHER FIGURE
- GUIDELINES
- LEADERSHIP
- ORDER
- ORGANIZATION
- PRINCIPLES
- RATIONAL THOUGHT
- REGULATION
- STABILITY
- STRUCTURE
- SYSTEMS

THE EMPEROR

- 4 -

```
R H V L R N L R E E G K C J W A T G H A
O C H B T R R Q L R C G L V U F F G U C
I M O Q H E V B E N U V E T R R K K R R
P I H S R E D A E L W T H O Q E P V B A
J B U E H I L B H L J O C P R R U U G T
T J S E Q T U F O K R R G U H G J U E I
W R K A R E V W R I B S E G R E R K W O
Q L E N S Z G S T G O W H D M T T I Y N
R E S G O N I Y E V T Q E A R U S E T A
M E U I U I F O H N T V A B O O H R I L
R I J V R L T C V E I E A O T H M U L T
O H G Q K M A I H W U L A R I O L G I H
I U J G S E T T B L E K E B R G R I B O
U C S C K G J H I M T C R D M C J F A U
D I R E C T I N G O A S E B I Z U R T G
N L I V K V Z O X L N J J H L U Q E S H
T Z L T S T S Y S T E M S W X S G H C T
D U V T N E M H S I L B A T S E K T L Q
B N O I T A Z I N A G R O F M C X A U P
P U I F V C P R I N C I P L E S V F E G
```

THE HIEROPHANT

- 5 -
EMPOWERMENT

Eventually, the Fool ventures out of his home into the wider world and craves knowledge. He is exposed to the beliefs and traditions of his culture and begins his formal education. The Hierophant represents the Fools spiritual father and organized belief systems that begin to surround and inform him. The Hierophant interprets arcane knowledge and mysteries. Although the image is religious, it is really a symbol of initiations of all kinds: spirit and matter, Gods and men. The Hierophant acts as the link between the two.

The child, trained in all the practices of his society, becomes part of a particular culture and worldview. He learns to identify with a group and discovers a sense of belonging. He enjoys learning the customs of his society and showing how well he can conform to them.

★ ★ ★

QUICK! JOT DOWN YOUR FIRST THOUGHTS ON THIS CARD.

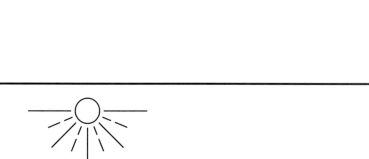

V

THE HIEROPHANT.

THE HIEROPHANT

Before you can discover your own belief systems and make your own choices, you need to learn fundamental principles such as those outlined by chosen sources such as society, religion, or even a mentor. This card suggests to embrace the traditions and conventions that surround you. You're unconsciously wanting to follow pre-established traditions with proven methods instead of trying some unorthodox methods. In short, find ways to identify with other like-minds to continue further learning.

LOCATE THE FOLLOWING WORDS IN THE WORDSEARCH ON THE NEXT PAGE:

- BELIEF SYSTEMS
- CONFORMITY
- CONVENTION
- EDUCATION
- FANATICISM
- FREEDOM
- GROUP IDENTIFICATION
- INSTITUTIONS
- TRADITION
- LEGACY
- PRINCIPLES
- RELIGION
- SOCIETY
- SPIRITUAL WISDOM
- STATUS QUO

THE HIEROPHANT

```
I E U N R W J R Q A I O Z J R B N D X X
F W S Z B U V I M M I D L E E J E K V F
V E N X D Z H I D H F K T L O C D K X P
T H O H E U L Q K I A A I A I T X I G R
N O I T A C I F I T N E D I P U O R G I
W T T O X A V F W J F H I V C E W U G N
A A U S S D J Q C S S O C I E T Y N U C
N Z T B Z X T M Y U I L B J L K Q A E I
J K I P O S O S S F N C G R V N C O U P
O B T X L P T U R I C S K T V X S C T L
H I S A S E U A Q E C T D K W W P G W E
F M N V M K T L N S L I O W V R I N A S
J W I S G J H N W U U I T M N S Z O W J
R I K V S M U F F F H T G A O Z O I Q Z
C O N F O R M I T Y W B A I N C E T W G
P L B V W D V L E G A C Y T O A X A B H
T R A D I T I O N T E T M I S N F C L K
C W X Q S C N O I T N E V N O C S U Z V
M O D S I W L A U T I R I P S B U D N A
K F M O D E E R F C K T I K C J W E A M
```

THE LOVERS

- 6 -
EMPOWERMENT

Love is one of the first trials of youth. Before, the Fool was mainly self-centered. Now he feels the balancing tendency to reach out and become half of a loving partnership, a conscious connection and a meaningful relationship with another person. He learns that he must be equal in the effort involved in a union.

The Lovers teach him that love is not a simple matter of physical and intuitive attraction, but is also the union of mental (male), emotional, (female) and spiritual (represented by the angel) levels. Lovers strive to balance forces. The Fool feels that he can continue his journey with the support of the Lover.

★ ★ ★

QUICK! JOT DOWN YOUR FIRST THOUGHTS ON THIS CARD.

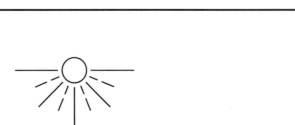

THE LOVERS.

THE LOVERS

- 6 -

This card is about being ready to establish your own belief system and decide what is essential to you, being authentic and genuine, staying true to yourself, and consciously choosing the connections you make. It can represent a romantic relationship, a close friendship, or a family relationship where love, respect, and compassion flow. Communicating openly and honestly (they are naked and vulnerable after all) can create a harmonious and fulfilling relationship built on trust and respect.

LOCATE THE FOLLOWING WORDS IN THE WORDSEARCH ON THE NEXT PAGE:

- AUTHENTIC
- CHOICE
- CONFLICT
- FRIENDS
- GENUINE
- HARMONY
- HONESTY
- LOVE
- MAGNETIC
- OPEN COMMUNICATION
- PERSONAL BELIEFS
- RELATIONSHIP
- SELF ESTEEM
- SEXUALITY
- VALUES

THE LOVERS

-6-

B	S	O	R	B	L	S	L	K	G	T	R	U	V	E	C	U	I	F	P
Q	I	O	N	O	I	T	A	C	I	N	U	M	M	O	C	N	E	P	O
D	S	G	Z	C	W	A	G	L	F	X	V	V	N	S	T	Z	Q	M	Q
D	T	L	T	W	X	S	C	T	H	O	A	F	T	E	B	A	V	I	D
Z	S	E	X	U	A	L	I	T	Y	Z	L	R	J	L	E	K	R	A	P
Z	Q	S	P	D	E	C	A	W	C	I	U	N	E	F	K	N	L	S	V
O	L	C	M	I	H	R	X	T	C	H	S	O	K	E	O	E	T	J	N
N	M	Q	I	O	H	M	H	T	C	H	Z	C	B	S	L	N	P	K	Z
C	O	T	I	T	J	S	A	L	Q	C	F	N	T	T	B	K	B	Z	K
X	W	C	J	I	N	H	N	G	O	B	R	B	J	E	F	Q	N	E	K
X	E	T	S	A	F	E	N	O	N	Y	E	T	Z	E	J	F	W	X	M
X	E	B	A	N	S	T	H	S	I	E	T	V	D	M	J	M	U	K	J
E	I	U	A	K	S	N	F	T	Z	T	T	S	A	H	Z	E	F	C	X
U	P	P	B	G	N	O	L	X	U	G	A	I	E	R	B	R	Y	V	L
F	R	I	E	N	D	S	X	T	U	A	V	L	C	N	D	Z	N	A	O
U	D	B	J	S	E	B	C	H	W	S	F	J	E	E	O	U	O	L	V
M	Z	S	G	D	D	C	G	I	B	F	P	U	U	R	J	H	M	U	E
D	F	U	P	B	T	M	K	C	E	N	I	U	N	E	G	P	R	E	J
S	F	E	I	L	E	B	L	A	N	O	S	R	E	P	D	M	A	S	R
H	H	U	U	Q	V	I	P	A	N	I	H	P	H	U	E	H	H	G	T

THE CHARIOT

- 7 -
EMPOWERMENT

The Fool must learn how to steer a middle course through the battleground of his opposing feelings, thoughts, and desires. This card brings forth the next trial of youth: conflict. As an adult, the Fool learns a strong identity and a certain mastery over himself. Through discipline and willpower, he has developed an inner control that allows him to triumph over his environment.

The Chariot represents the vigorous ego that is the Fool's crowning achievement so far. We witness a proud, commanding figure riding victoriously through his world, in visible control of himself and all he surveys. The struggles were draining, but the success was worth it. He is the assured confidence of youth. He is stronger and has gained empowerment to continue his journey.

The first stage of his journey is complete. He has received the benefits of his education with his teacher and parents; he has learned lessons in love and war. He is now ready to learn the four moral lessons namely, Justice, Temperance, Strength and Prudence (The Hermit).

★ ★ ★

QUICK! JOT
DOWN YOUR
FIRST
THOUGHTS ON
THIS CARD.

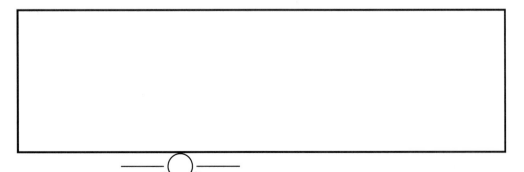

THE CHARIOT.

THE CHARIOT

With your decisions now in alignment with your values from the Lover's card, the action begins. You have the dedication now to make things happen if you maintain control. You have the strength, willpower, and confidence to maintain your focus, confidence, and determination through everything you're facing. Once you have a solid plan, you will have a structured approach to ensure that you meet whatever goals you're reaching for. Keep your focus and remain confident in your ability and assert yourself - victory is within reach.

LOCATE THE FOLLOWING WORDS IN THE WORDSEARCH ON THE NEXT PAGE:

- ACTION
- ASSERTION
- COMMITMENT
- CONFIDENCE
- DETERMINATION
- DRIVING
- ENCOURAGEMENT
- FOCUS
- PASSION
- SELF-CONTROL
- SELF-DISCIPLINE
- STRENGTH
- SUCCESS
- VICTORY
- WILLPOWER

THE CHARIOT

```
V  V  X  G  K  P  S  A  A  D  G  H  C  R  E  A  W  N  C  D
Q  C  F  M  L  U  J  X  X  J  N  V  H  S  S  G  V  B  R  S
C  K  G  R  H  T  L  R  V  S  Z  F  N  S  R  S  Z  E  H  D
W  S  W  L  P  A  U  Z  M  K  M  L  E  P  F  K  W  N  X  J
J  E  N  R  N  L  N  J  X  K  I  R  E  Q  J  O  V  Q  K  S
Z  L  P  O  N  O  G  J  Z  O  T  G  X  D  P  W  G  Q  X  Q
P  F  Y  L  I  W  I  V  C  I  F  Z  U  L  D  H  B  H  S  S
U  D  R  B  J  S  W  T  O  L  I  O  L  H  E  T  U  L  Q  K
I  I  O  A  A  S  S  N  A  Z  I  I  C  S  P  G  S  G  W  N
X  S  T  Z  E  N  E  A  W  N  W  G  Z  U  M  N  C  J  B  N
S  C  C  J  C  L  O  L  P  R  I  H  G  O  S  E  W  E  H  V
S  I  I  I  G  A  F  I  F  E  O  M  J  B  U  R  E  C  G  F
E  P  V  S  B  P  S  Q  T  C  X  Z  R  D  Q  T  R  N  W  I
C  L  Z  L  V  B  N  Z  V  C  O  P  C  E  J  S  L  E  K  M
C  I  D  U  D  W  O  I  H  K  A  N  L  G  T  V  U  D  A  Q
U  N  G  H  T  F  J  Q  W  G  N  G  T  O  P  E  I  I  E  M
S  E  C  M  D  G  W  G  N  K  V  S  B  R  P  I  D  F  Z  W
I  H  S  U  B  H  T  N  E  M  T  I  M  M  O  C  V  N  S  F
T  N  E  M  E  G  A  R  U  O  C  N  E  G  Z  L  G  O  K  N
H  E  G  N  I  V  I  R  D  B  B  U  D  R  V  A  G  C  N  W
```

STRENGTH

- 8 -
TRANSFORMATION

Over time, life presents the Fool with new challenges, some of which cause suffering and disillusionment. He has many occasions to draw on the quality of Strength. He is pressed to develop his courage and resolve and find the heart to keep going despite setbacks.

The Fool also discovers the quiet attributes of patience and tolerance. He realizes the willful command of the Chariot (outer strength and will) must be tempered by kindness and the softer power of a loving approach (inner strength and the ability to overcome obstacles). At times, intense passions surface, just when the Fool thought he had everything, including himself, under control. He must resist the urge to react with raw emotions.

The Fool must now practice control and use his thoughts and feelings correctly. Strength to hold his tongue. The inner will to soften external outbursts.

★ ★ ★

QUICK! JOT DOWN YOUR FIRST THOUGHTS ON THIS CARD.

VIII

STRENGTH.

STRENGTH

- 8 -

Your strength gives you confidence and this card encourages you to find the power within. Your advantage is that you are underestimated; you can quietly influence and persuade others rather than use outward force. When navigating tough times, you remain strong and courageous and are able to bear trouble calmly. You are resilient and fearless and can accomplish anything you set your mind to.

LOCATE THE FOLLOWING WORDS IN THE WORDSEARCH ON THE NEXT PAGE:

- COMPOSURE
- COMPASSION
- CONVICTION
- COURAGE
- DETERMINATION
- ENDURE OBSTACLES
- GRACEFUL
- INFLUENCE
- INNER STRENGTH
- PATIENCE
- PERSEVERE
- PERSISTENCE
- PERSONAL POWER
- PERSUASION
- STRONG

STRENGTH

- 8 -

```
H S R I N F L U E N C E U M E C U I F G
P I I D K G X M X F Q M G Z O U U O C X
T X L S S I O B E L T P G M A E G J A E
U H G S A K E J J Z N P Z Q N E S N C
S Z V B N U N A K F C O K T O R H D V F
L N Z E W O J D W D S H L R E F U Z O O
E I O B C P I S X U K S T V R R E H N O
C Q L I S N E T R W N S E C E D T K O E
N O H F S A E E A C R S R O C G J Q I B
E N B L P S A I S N R D B K N G R H S V
T L R U V S A T T E I S O E H L M S A B
S O Q F R F J P P A T M R V L F X M U M
I L P E G K N X M A P T R C Z D I O S Z
S J A C N M B A C O S H R E M V E E R Q
R Q J A J Z O L G R C X D W T G R G E X
E R P R L W E V E D Z C G D K E T A P V
P C D G J S X N M O Z M Q I B A D R P L
M L N F R V N O I T C I V N O C J U Z Q
A E O Z J I A M D B Z G U A D K O O O W
R E W O P L A N O S R E P Q B P Q C Z N
```

THE HERMIT

- 9 -

TRANSFORMATION

Sooner or later, the Fool is led to ask himself the age-old question "Why?" He becomes absorbed with the search for answers, not from idle curiosity, but out of a deeply felt need to find out why people live if only to suffer and die. The Hermit represents the need to find deeper truth.

The Hermit symbolizes the withdrawal of the Fool from the outside world and into the quiet inner one. He teaches the Fool solitude (one of mans greatest) fears.

The Fool begins to look inward, trying to understand his feelings and motivations. The sensual world holds less attraction for him, and he seeks moments of solitude away from the frantic activity of society. In time he may seek a teacher or guide who can give him advice and direction. He has become one with the Hermit.

⋆ ⋆ ⋆

QUICK! JOT DOWN YOUR FIRST THOUGHTS ON THIS CARD.

IX

THE HERMIT.

THE HERMIT

- 9 -

This card asks you to draw your energy and attention inward and find the answers you are seeking within your soul. Your inner wisdom is your guiding light. Retreat into your private world for introspection. If you are at a pivotal point in your life or are contemplating the trappings of society that no longer serve you, take a break, and turn inward with contemplation, meditation, and self-examination where you will find the innermost knowledge of yourself.

LOCATE THE FOLLOWING WORDS IN THE WORDSEARCH ON THE NEXT PAGE:

- BEING ALONE
- CONTEMPLATION
- DELIBERATION
- INNER GUIDANCE
- INSIGHT
- INTROSPECTION
- LIFE REVIEW
- RETREAT
- SELF-AWARENESS
- SERVICE
- SEARCHING
- SOLITUDE
- SOUL-SEARCHING
- TEACHING
- THINKING

THE HERMIT

- 9 -

```
S S V S O L I T U D E D H M O C H X B D
F E U P Z T L U B N U C K J O O G V V G
G L C T F Q D S O Q U B I N J I L G C S
J N M I K Q A F J K Q O T A N N N C E G
G R I W V Q D B G K J E M C H I L L V G
N E G H P R K L G N M V H A K Z F N G S
I N N H C Q E W M P I L G N G A W E D V
H B T O D R N S L V N H I M W J T E S B
C W I B L O A A F Q Q H C A I B G C N C
R T O S W A T E C H T B R A T R R N Q T
A K W G K I G I S N T E F P E Z A A V F
E W E K O B I N W D N H I X U T G D E E
S T I N L E K R I E I R G E S V G I X W
L S V I S B P O S E B U G I J R O U U F
U L E J A D B S M Z B V J E S B B G B D
O A R W A N V T O B C I M W R N H R F G
S M E O B K Q I F I M I L K E Q I E A R
T F F V N O I T A R E B I L E D E N X N
N O I T C E P S O R T N I M A H W N R P
W B L K W P R E T R E A T V D B S I T J
```

FIND THE DIFFERENCE

CAN YOU FIND THE DIFFERENCES
BETWEEN THESE TWO IMAGES?

THERE ARE 21 DIFFERENCES

TAROT TILES

REBUILD THE SENTENCE OR PHRASE

T_r_t c_rds d_p_nd _n s_mb_l_sm _nd
N_m_r_l_g_ d_p_nds _n n_mb_rs wh_ch m__ s__nd
s_mpl_ b_t _r_ _ct__ll_ c_mpl_x s_st_ms _f
d_v_n_t__n.

HINT: DIFFERENCES

_____

_____

_____

_____

_____

_____

_____

_____

MISSING VOWELS

Can you rebuild the phrase? Fill in the missing vowels to complete
the phrase.

HIDDEN OBJECT

CAN YOU FIND THE SWORD IN THE PICTURE?

NUMEROLOGY TILES

REBUILD THE SENTENCE OR PHRASE

N_m_r_l_g_ _s th_ b_l__f _n _ d_v_n_ _r m_st_c_l
r_l_t__nsh_p b_tw__n _ n_mb_r _nd _n_ _r m_r_
c__nc_d_ng _v_nts.

HINT: RELATIONSHIPS

_____

_____

_____

_____

_____

_____

_____

_____

_____

_____

MISSING VOWELS

Can you rebuild the phrase? Fill in the missing vowels to complete the phrase.

WHEEL OF FORTUNE

- 10 -

TRANSFORMATION

After much soul-searching, the Fool begins to see how everything connects. He has a vision of the world's wondrous design; its intricate patterns and cycles. He understands there is more to life than him and the external world. The Wheel of Fortune is a symbol of the mysterious universe whose parts work together in harmony. When the Fool glimpses the beauty and order of the world if only briefly, he finds some of the answers he is seeking.

Sometimes his experiences seemed to be the work of fate. He sees his destiny in the sequence of events that led him to this turning point. Having been solitary, he feels ready for movement and action again. His perspective is wider, and he sees himself within the grander scheme of a universal plan. His sense of purpose is restored.

He understands both stability and change, the external, changing world, that fate moves the circumference of the wheel, that each man is responsible for his destiny and that although circumstances are determined, man has ultimate control over how he deals with them. He now knows "this too shall pass" and that nothing is permanent.

★ ★ ★

QUICK! JOT DOWN YOUR FIRST THOUGHTS ON THIS CARD.

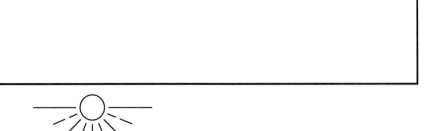

WHEEL of FORTUNE.

WHEEL OF FORTUNE

- 10 -

This card is about balancing good times and bad times. Life is in a state of constant change. Cherish the good times as the cycle will soon turn, remember them to carry you through the bad times. Practice karma: what you give you will receive because the Universe listens. Be willing to grow and expand and keep an open mind to the miracles happening. Don't try to control. Instead, accept and adapt and go with the flow. Unexpected and unusual opportunities may present themselves if you keep an open mind. Allowing the universe and your intuition to guide you could reward you with outcomes you also didn't expect.

LOCATE THE FOLLOWING WORDS IN THE WORDSEARCH ON THE NEXT PAGE:

- CHANGING
- CURVE BALLS
- DESTINY
- EXPANSION
- GOOD FORTUNE
- HARMONY
- KARMA
- LIFE CYCLES
- LUCK
- MOVEMENT
- PERSONAL VISION
- TIMING
- TURNING POINT
- UNEXPECTED PROBLEMS
- UNEXPECTED REWARDS

WHEEL OF FORTUNE

- 10 -

```
W B Z O A G C F S J P S Q X C C Q Q W F
Z L V J M T Z U O W L H J C G I X I U P
U W B D F U U P R B T K H U M H B K N T
Q G F I V G V R I V G B M D G V P M E I
T J T E S B N I N B E O G H Q O O F X M
N L N N H Z D Q I I J B F O S X X W P I
E A O U R M F W O O N J A L M H W U E N
M E I T Y N I T S E D G R L G H D A C G
E V S R X B O H T E T L P E L K K M T A
V L I O P C A I R T D T A O W S C R E B
O I V F P E H N S J G N X B I N G A D M
M F L D A X K A L N H A R M O N Y K P O
L E A O P T M B N G A G F J W A T B R T
E C N O E G H K F G T P I X P D F R O D
G Y O G P K M C K Z I Z X L Q X L W B K
Z C S D T F C L H S J W E M S W T L E
G L R P T T A U J H Z A G P S O D I E Q
N E E N M Q L L P Z K K T N P K Z M N
U S P O T M Z S N W I R R K K A U H S Z
F S D R A W E R D E T C E P X E N U T C
```

JUSTICE

- 11 -
TRANSFORMATION

Justice teaches the Fool to discriminate, to make dispassionate evaluations and impersonal decisions. Think with a clear and balanced mind. He looks back over his life to trace the cause-and-effect relationships that have brought him to this point. He takes responsibility for his past actions so he can make amends and ensure a more honest course for the future. The demands of Justice must be served so that he can wipe the slate clean.

This is a time of decision for the Fool. He is making important choices. Will he remain true to his insights, or will he slip back into an easier, more unaware existence that closes off further growth? He knows actions have consequences, both good and bad. Everyone will be held responsible for their actions.

★ ★ ★

QUICK! JOT DOWN YOUR FIRST THOUGHTS ON THIS CARD.

XI

JUSTICE.

JUSTICE

- 11 -

With this card, you may be called to account for your actions. But Justice is compassionate, understanding, unbiased, and acts fairly. This card ultimately means that the truth behind everything will come to light soon and there will be repercussions for the wrongdoer. You may be on a search for truth, but everything is not always as clear-cut as we'd like them to be and sometimes the water gets muddy. If you need to make an important decision, connect with your intuition and ask for the answer that benefits your highest self, stand by your decisions and accept the consequences.

LOCATE THE FOLLOWING WORDS IN THE WORDSEARCH ON THE NEXT PAGE:

- BALANCING
- CAUSE AND EFFECT
- COMPASSION
- CONSEQUENCES
- DECISION MAKING
- EQUALITY
- FAIRNESS
- HARMONY
- INEQUALITY
- JUSTICE
- LAW
- RESPONSIBILITY
- RULING
- TRUTH
- UNBIASED

JUSTICE

- 11 -

```
A A Z I S X E G W D W U A Y E C W U R F
L U Z G U A C J E O Y O T W A W H M T T
B T C N V N M S J T T I I U K J P S Q E
X C K G W X A I I M L B S S E Q T U F C
O R P P N I N L R I J E W E H T U R T I
W H O H B I A K B L A G V H A R N H T T
N J G N Q U K I W N G M F M F E M T E S
N C U N Q M S A D D G A W P N K V S U
B P I E I N B E M O G J I R O U F S L J
H A N I O C F R I N K G R L U S X E Z X
A I R P N F N R F M O M N V U X Z C T D
N J S U E N P A E M Q I E X O R L N T M
D E T C C B S H L R K M S E M S P E A X
R R T O N J G N X A B P S I H M A U X K
L U L P T N B G H G B L Z I C C T Q I E
G Y N O M R A H J K F T I Z P E D E G R
D G P M C L T T F K R C P C R E D S M E
D U C X G E N O I S S A P M O C M N Q N
V U R V W I L J A E W A L P S U D O I R
N Y T I L A U Q E P N Q B F K T D C D V
```

HANGED MAN

- 12 -

TRANSFORMATION

Undaunted, the Fool pushes on. He is determined to realize his vision, but he finds life is not so easily tamed. Sooner or later, he encounters his personal cross - an experience that seems too difficult to endure. This overwhelming challenge humbles him until he has no choice but to give up and let go. His journey hangs in limbo as a result of indecision.

The Fool feels defeated and lost. He believes he has sacrificed everything, but from the depths, he learns an amazing truth. He finds that when he relinquishes his struggle for control, everything begins to work as it should. By becoming open and vulnerable, the Fool discovers the miraculous support of his Inner Self. He learns to surrender to his experiences, rather than fighting them. He feels a surprising joy and begins to flow with life.

The Fool feels suspended in a timeless moment, free of urgency and pressure. In truth, his world has been turned upside-down. The Fool is the Hanged Man, apparently martyred, but actually serene and at peace.

★ ★ ★

QUICK! JOT DOWN YOUR FIRST THOUGHTS ON THIS CARD.

THE HANGED MAN.

HANGED MAN

- 12 -

You might be feeling stuck or restricted, or maybe you're just pushing through to finish a project. This card reminds us to take pause before taking another step. Release old models and behaviors for a new pattern to emerge. Surrender to the opportunity to see a new perspective. Embrace opportunities that you might have overlooked. Tune into your intuition to know when to take this pause - or the Universe will do it for you. Take a break from what you're doing and put it aside or change your routine to allow your energy to shift and flow more freely.

LOCATE THE FOLLOWING WORDS IN THE WORDSEARCH ON THE NEXT PAGE:

- ALIGNMENT
- BREAK
- DREAMS
- EMBRACE
- ILLUSION
- LETTING GO
- NEW PERSPECTIVE
- OPPORTUNITY
- PAUSE
- RELEASE
- REST
- REVERSAL
- SLOW DOWN
- SURRENDER
- SUSPENSION

HANGED MAN

- 12 -

```
N P C S U S P E N S I O N G S D X Q R F
B C B D A O D E M V O X A V R F W K E J
I V C I W U G E A P S S D E J R C N D A
K L I E F I E X D A C P A G M Q N T N U
U M A N V T C W J U S M G K V T W K E H
H G K S U I B E B S S D A F H J D R S
F X T N R R T L D E Q L F N T K C A R A
L Z B N E E K C O J B D S L K G R Q U O
L A O A E S V E E C F N A R E D K G S Z
C N K A G M L E C P E P V E V T X N K P
B J J S V Q N O R L S A M S H O S T B S
V I D Q Z R J G W Z H R G T X M W O P R
B R X W C U N E I D K G E D K V O G L D
K X T H H E J L Q L O K I P F G F G H V
E M B R A C E A O R A W Z Z W C F N G B
Q A V L B C P B D L K B N J Z E Z I K P
W J T H W B R B J F Q F S K Q T N T R X
C N S T D S P B N O I S U L L I C T W A
G L Y T I N U T R O P P O F X V V E T X
P S W B R J R E L E A S E S M Z T L D T
```

DEATH

- 13 -
TRANSFORMATION

During the pause of the Hanged Man, Death arrives telling to Fool to "Let it be and release yourself from old ways." It's the death of the ego. The Fool now begins to eliminate old habits and tired approaches. He cuts out nonessentials because he appreciates the basics of life. He goes through endings as he puts the outgrown aspects of his life behind him.

His process may seem like dying because it is the death of his familiar self, which allows for the growth of a new one. At times this inexorable change seems to be crushing the Fool, but eventually, he rises up to discover that death is not a permanent state. It is simply a transition to a new, more fulfilling way of life. Death card strips him bare of all his pretentions and leaves him naked for his next lesson.

★ ★ ★

QUICK! JOT DOWN YOUR FIRST THOUGHTS ON THIS CARD.

DEATH.

DEATH

- 13 -

The Death Card is one of the most feared cards in the Major Arcana deck because it's misunderstood. This card simply means that one phase of your life has ended and the next one is going to begin. Death shows a time of significant transformation, change, and transition. Closing the door on the past only to open a door to the future. Even if you're scared of what's to come, you will find that the future holds bigger and better things for you. Realize what is no longer serving you, and open up to the possibility of something far more valuable and essential. Let go of unhealthy attachments in your life to pave the way to a fuller, more fulfilled life of deeper meaning and significance, let go of outworn and outgrown ways of life, break a bad habit or pattern of behavior, or cut out excess and unnecessary things in your life. Purge the old belongings, memories, and baggage that are getting in your way.

LOCATE THE FOLLOWING WORDS IN THE WORDSEARCH ON THE NEXT PAGE:

- BAGGAGE
- CHANGE
- DEATH OF THE EGO
- ELIMINATION
- ENDING
- FULFILLING
- INEXORABLE FORCES
- INITIATION
- LET GO
- OPPORTUNITY
- PHASE
- PURGE
- START OVER
- TRANSFORMATION
- TRANSITION

DEATH

- 13 -

```
X D L I N I T I A T I O N D C D O K K X
F M P M T O U M N S C W J R E G K V A T
Y H N O I T A M R O F S N A R T F F D I
H T O D U S D A D G J D T S D W N L N L
D Q I K F N T J J B X H J W O R G E E R
J L A N T R C P R Z O X G S C G X T D L
M V D D U H K E Q F M O J T B O G N P L
F X I I A T V G T I U W E R R O W H J R
Q A I N E O R H N O Z G J A S N A D Z A
J A G T T G E O I I R D B Q Z S R J Z H
G E X R M E A W P U L L N Q E B Q X T U
I L A Z G J N G P P E L D K T I L D J X
T T G O H E J L G F O Q I K I D D C F T
S X E Z B B C F O A G B Q F A V L B C P
U D L K O H W R W H B M T G L R P G V B
Q B J F P F C S J Q S R X V O U D N F K
Z V H J I E B E B A N L L K M D F I H M
W H G Q S N O I T A N I M I L E K D M H
W J A Z P K W Q K S Z P P H H X I N F V
C V D P W T R A N S I T I O N P N E K V
```

TEMPERANCE

- 14 -
TRANSFORMATION

Since embracing the Hermit, the Fool has swung wildly back and forth on an emotional pendulum. The Fool has learned the value of a balanced mind and he must now complement this with a balanced heart. He arrives at Temperance with her calm waters and decides to rest where he realizes the balancing stability of temperance. He discovers true poise, grace and equilibrium. By experiencing the extremes, he has come to appreciate moderation.

Temperance offers to teach the Fool compassion and forgiveness, taking into account the feelings in situations rather than just facts and circumstances. He welcomes this sense of calm and serenity, the equivalent of what the mind knows as Justice.

The Fool now has a clear vision of his goals. He has the earthly tools and guidance to enter into enlightenment.

★ ★ ★

QUICK! JOT DOWN YOUR FIRST THOUGHTS ON THIS CARD.

XIV

TEMPERANCE.

TEMPERANCE

14

Temperance is the card for bringing balance, patience, and moderation into your life. This card means that when you're going through troubled, anxious, dark times, you have not fallen. You have been calm and when helping others, you take the middle road as the peacekeeper with a balanced and moderate approach. Practice alchemy - blend, mix, and combine diverse elements in a way that creates something new and even more valuable than its separate parts.

Reflect on your priorities and create a clear long-term vision. Don't rush. Stabilize your energy and allow the life force to flow through without force or resistance. Recover your flow and get your life back into order and balance.

LOCATE THE FOLLOWING WORDS IN THE WORDSEARCH ON THE NEXT PAGE:

- ALCHEMY
- BALANCE
- CALM
- COMBINATION
- COMPROMISE
- COOPERATION
- GUIDED APPROACH
- HARMONY
- MODERATION
- ORDER
- PATIENCE
- PURPOSE
- STABILIZE
- TEMPERANCE
- UNION

TEMPERANCE

-14-

```
L A D O V O Y K L X K M V E J C Q J U R
O O H E G N R I U Q U H D P A M A J W S
Q W C L O X Q D W F B T T L J V O D I G
Q V W M V X H L E P C K M K S V E X U S
C L R G I R S U R R T A X N W Z G I G W
E A D V B T B D N O P N V R I I D S U W
H I B O E A N F Q A O D F L K E Z V H J
I B M R L S L O T O E E I A D O V Z I H
X X C A Y E O I I A V B F A W K T J I W
D I N X U M E P G T A E P E N T E T F K
R C D P C N E R R T A P E O K C M E B I
E J G T C K J H S U R R I M K R P S E E
J K Q E O S F P C O P T E C G S E I W W
L H J K B I B A L A T F P U E R M F H
J D S F X P M C F R A R L N O G A O T A
Q Q J U Q O H G E P D N I F H O N R X Q
P L W T C Q U D C O G O H Q O O C P F L
H Z D P A N O I T A N I B M O C E M H D
I Q V W V M X P L P H Q P Z E I X O H Q
M C X Z G W A C J V O W N O M L A C P A
```

THE DEVIL

- 15 -

ENLIGHTENMENT

On his path the enlightenment, the Fool soon comes face to face with the Devil. The Devil tricks the fool into thinking enlightenment has already happened and tempts him with earthly vices. He offers him everything he wants if he only stays with the Devil.

The Devil is not an evil, sinister figure residing outside of us. He is the knot of ignorance and hopelessness lodged within each of us at some level. The seductive attractions of the material world bind us so compellingly that we often do not even realize our slavery to them.

The couple on the card are chained, but acquiescent. They could easily free themselves, but they do not even apprehend their bondage. Like the Fool, they do not realize there are no ties that they cannot remove themselves.

The Devil is symbolic of repressed fears which, once removed, can release positive energy. In this lesson the Fool learns to accept all aspects of his nature i.e. both the good and the bad.

★ ★ ★

QUICK! JOT DOWN YOUR FIRST THOUGHTS ON THIS CARD.

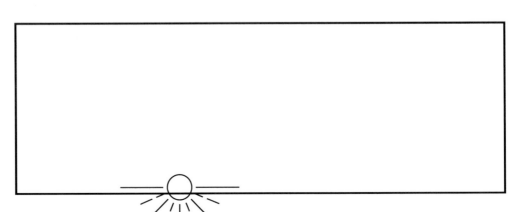

THE DEVIL.

THE DEVIL

- 15 -

The Devil card represents your shadow side and the negative forces that constrain you and hold you back from being the best version of yourself. This card means that you're feeling trapped somehow. It could be at work, at home with your family, or in your marriage, negative habits, dependencies, behaviors, thought patterns, relationships, or addictions. You maybe feel like you have no power to change. Acknowledge and take action to begin to free yourself. Open your eyes to the situation you're in and see if you're truly powerless. Once you realize this, you can start making positive changes in your life to free yourself from the shackles life has locked you in.

LOCATE THE FOLLOWING WORDS IN THE WORDSEARCH ON THE NEXT PAGE:

- ABUSE
- ADDICTION
- ATTACHMENT
- BONDAGE
- CODEPENDENCY
- FACING YOUR FEAR
- FINDING BALANCE
- FREEDOM
- HOPELESSNESS
- IGNORANCE
- MATERIALISM
- RESTRICTION
- SEXUALITY
- SHADOW SELF
- TEMPTATION

THE DEVIL

```
S F N M E W Z A V F P K U V W A D T X G
M Z B F Z C R C Q P U V U W D Z K S Z B
I H G T L B N Q M K Q A F D P M H E N F
E Z L M U E M A Q V P W I I I S E X O I
N R V J Q Q S Z R E O C Z J C I O U T N
R J K W J Y L W T O R H M P L U A N D I
T A U Q V I C N O I N A N O E A H L O I
X E E H P U L N O D B G P D F I L I I N
P M M F T O H N E M A N I E S R C T T G
O Q R P R G K V A D T H H E F E S Y C B
S M D H T U E M W H N G S R Q T K M I A
H W J A Z A O S P H T E N F J A R X R L
M S C D T Z T Y U B R O P R U M L S T A
L K G R P I S I G B A I A E C M S E S N
B B H V K E G Z O N A O K P D J E G E C
Z Z X A R N R F V N I M T W X O S A R E
C T H I A T U A T I D C Z Z Q W C D H V
I G A I T W T N E M H C A T T A G N U I
Z F D R O N R P W X B P P F V E X O K T
I S S E N S S E L E P O H K V R L B U F
```

THE TOWER

- 16 -

ENLIGHTENMENT

The Fool can release himself from the Devil through sudden change and massive destruction, represented by the Tower. It's the final shattering of earthly illusions. The Tower is the ego fortress each of us has built around his beautiful inner core. Gray, cold, and rock-hard, this fortress seems to protect but it is really a prison.

Sometimes only a monumental crisis can generate enough power to smash the walls of a Tower. The lightning bolt striking this building (representing spiritual truth) has ejected the occupants who seem to be tumbling to their deaths. The crown (representing material life) tumbles from it's thrust of power; now they are humbled by a force stronger than they are.

The Fool may need such a severe shakeup to realize he cannot control chaos. He lets go of what he cannot control and watches to see where the pieces may fall. The dark despair is blasted away in an instant, and the light of truth is free to shine down. He knows that sometimes things must fall apart to make room for re-birth.

★ ★ ★

QUICK! JOT
DOWN YOUR
FIRST
THOUGHTS ON
THIS CARD.

THE TOWER.

THE TOWER

16

This card tells you to expect the unexpected – massive change, upheaval, destruction, and chaos. Any event that shakes you to your core, affects you spiritually, mentally, and/or physically. There's no escaping it. Change is here to tear things up, create chaos and destroy everything in its path. Don't despair, it's for your Highest Good. This card is a reminder that change is a natural thing in life, and it's one that we must embrace. Keep your faith; you will find what works best for you. Over time, you will see that your original beliefs were built on a false understanding, and your new belief systems are more representative of reality. Surrender no matter how painful or unwanted. In the end, you will be stronger, wiser, and more resilient.

LOCATE THE FOLLOWING WORDS IN THE WORDSEARCH ON THE NEXT PAGE:

- ACCIDENT
- ACTS OF GOD
- AWAKENING
- CHAOS
- DANGER
- DESTRUCTION
- DOWNFALL
- FALSE UNDERSTANDING
- RELEASE
- REVELATION
- SUDDEN CHANGE
- SURRENDER
- TRAUMA
- UNEXPECTED
- UPHEAVAL

THE TOWER

-16-

```
C O K J W D S T R Z M V C A B A P M F O
U S S U D H B V A A Z I L P C T G P A N
X U A Z T D V Q H E I K E T O H F A L C
R D R S D J Q B N B P A S K T A B E S H
E D I L B H L J Q A D O R H R J P I E A
V E M N B F R V P D F U E B A U C U U D
E N H R C C N M G G H C L R U D W V N K
L C D T P D K O O D M S E J M J U B D R
A H T E N N E D I Z M E A G A U N G E F
T A B M L E Z T P T V Z S W P O J J R V
I N W I L U D X C B C V E H Z F Q K S I
O G A A A I T I P E T U E G W N X A T E
N E W G Q C Z W C P P A R E V Q Z U A T
T M D T C K S H S C V X K T M E V S N P
A W A K E N I N G A A B E U S N A R D K
N L S T I L L R L X T G Q N E E J E I T
Q K I D B U D A V A M V T O U B D G N C
I M V R H E O K E O H S O A H C N N G B
J B Z K W W R E D N E R R U S N C A N F
H L L A F N W O D X H P L V T C P D O Z
```

FIND THE DIFFERENCE

CAN YOU FIND THE DIFFERENCES
BETWEEN THESE TWO IMAGES?

THERE ARE 33 DIFFERENCES

DESIGN YOUR OWN

THE TOWER CARD IS ABOUT CHANGE: ONE CYCLE ENDING SO THE NEXT CAN BEGIN. THE IMAGE ON THE CARD IS NOT THE MOST FAVORABLE. HOW WOULD YOU DRAW THIS CARD ABOUT CHANGE?

THE STAR

- 17 -
ENLIGHTENMENT

The Fool is suffused with a serene calm. The beautiful images of the Star attest to this tranquility. The woman pictured on this card is naked, her soul no longer hidden behind any disguise. Radiant stars shine in a cloudless sky serving as a beacon of hope and inspiration. She represents the truth unveiled and there is nothing to hide or fear.

The Star offers the Fool optimism and hope along his difficult path, as well as inspiration. He is blessed with a trust that completely replaces the negative energies of the Devil. The destruction of the Tower is silenced by inspiration. His faith in himself and hope for the future is restored. He is filled with joy and his one wish is to share it generously with the rest of the world. His heart is open, and his love pours out freely. This peace after the storm is a magical moment for the Fool.

★ ★ ★

QUICK! JOT
DOWN YOUR
FIRST
THOUGHTS ON
THIS CARD.

THE STAR.

THE STAR

- 17 -

This card comes as a welcome reprieve after a period of destruction and turmoil. When you pull The Star card, it means that you have renewed your strength to carry on in life, and magic is flowing around you. This card is a reminder to have faith; you will go through any challenge in life and come out still having hope and faith in yourself. Appreciate all that you have. You are entering a peaceful, loving phase in your life, filled with calm energy, mental stability, and a more in-depth understanding of both yourself and the others around you. Allow yourself to dream, to aspire, to elevate in any way possible so you can reach the stars.

LOCATE THE FOLLOWING WORDS IN THE WORDSEARCH ON THE NEXT PAGE:

- COMMUNITY
- DEVELOPMENT
- GENEROSITY
- GROWTH
- HARMONY
- HELP
- HOPE
- INSPIRATION
- OPTIMISM
- PURPOSE
- RENEWED FAITH
- SERENITY
- SPIRITUALITY
- TRANSPARENCY
- PEACEFUL

THE STAR

- 17 -

```
B O I R W I E U W R P W J R Q D A I O Z
J R N D X A G X A D K E W W E P M I L K
E Q A S V E F V E X D Y A V C Q I M H S
F M W U M S F L Z W C J E C K I K M P R
L U F F D O H F J N M L U H E H R I S V
Q U J D J P O G E S O F H P N F R D L A
A L Y Q Z R K R V P K X D S D I U K G R
H V L T X U A E M Z B L T Z T Z U L N L
I O R V I P C E H B T Q R U Q S K N Q A
L L T P S N N Q N O I T A R I P S N I L
A M H N U T U O S L Y L X S M V E R Q J
J Z A O U G X M K I I N M W O X V R I E
K R U G P K H P M T Z Z O H H N E Q B K
T O C N S E M U Y O I I E M U W R W J H
Z Q A I O Z J B S K C H U M R P K H R E
M S I M I T P O X N N M D T C A K T S L
Q A R A L D C O K H O L A O E D H W F P
I K L Q W S Y T I S O R E N E G N O X D
Q H T I A F D E W E N E R C O X L R R R
Q S K G K I S E R E N I T Y F F P G Q S
```

THE MOON

- 18 -
ENLIGHTENMENT

What effect could spoil this perfect calm? Is there another challenge for the Fool? In fact, it is his bliss that makes him vulnerable to the illusions of the Moon. The Fool's joy is a feeling state. His positive emotions are not yet subject to mental clarity. In his dreamy condition, the Fool is susceptible to fantasy, distortion, and a false picture of the truth. The Moon tells him there is still much to learn.

The Moon stimulates the creative imagination. It opens the way for bizarre and beautiful thoughts to bubble up from the unconscious, but deep-seated fears and anxieties still arise. These experiences may cause the Fool to feel lost and bewildered. He wakes one night in the shadow of the Moon and realizes he needs to purge negative self-talk and leave it behind. The Moon symbolizes the upward progress of man, shining light on his path.

QUICK! JOT DOWN YOUR FIRST THOUGHTS ON THIS CARD.

THE MOON.

THE MOON

18

This card projects your fears and illusions and shows up when you may be projecting something from your past into your current or future possibilities. Previous emotions that were pushed down are bubbling up to the surface. It's time to release those fears and anxieties. This may be a time of illusion and uncertainty where nothing is as it seems and only part of the information is being revealed. Tune in and trust your intuition and allow it to guide you. Feel rather than think. The Moon's light will bring you clarity and knowledge that will guide you through these tough times, and into the light where you will find peace and understanding.

LOCATE THE FOLLOWING WORDS IN THE WORDSEARCH ON THE NEXT PAGE:

- ANXIETY
- AWARENESS
- DELUSION
- DREAMS
- EMOTIONS
- FANTASY
- FEAR
- ILLUSION
- IMAGINATION
- INSIGHTS
- INTUITION
- RELEASE
- SECRETS
- SUBCONSCIOUS
- UNCERTAINTY

THE MOON

- 18 -

```
F G A U N C E R T A I N T Y O A K P J E
Q R Q S B G K T F D N N H K W F T G X W
M F R L G S P V K K C C T A S X G X D W
G Q X Q P T L W V C Z U R U D B H S S U
B H V K E E G X E H M E G Z I W W V Z P
L P C S K R T V X S N C T G I T A S G U
A C J O O C W N O E M T I R I T I W G O
I Z F D R E F T S X V T V U M N S O Z V
J R I K Y S V S R L O F T S V M J M N U
H H Q K L T G W N O I T A N I G A M I U
A R G E S A E L E R Y H T G J R W F M F
E M A A L U L I C C S S C B I J G T C R
M K R E F R K Q X O E N A P C P S S X U
S X Z X A J N R F N M M V T X A V N F F
D E L U S I O N N J A U T V N C T O T E
S T H G I S N I I S H Q U U Q A V I I A
P A N I J X J P L W M A Q W A X F T N R
X Z I O F S P C D W S M A E R D A O G L
F S U O I C S N O C B U S Z V V V M X P
S N O I S U L L I O J Z Q Z S V Q E U R
```

THE SUN

- 19 -
ENLIGHTENMENT

It is the lucid clarity of the Sun that directs the Fool's imagination and renews his faith in his journey. The Sun's illumination shines in all the hidden places. It dispels the clouds of confusion and fear. It enlightens, so the Fool both feels and understands the goodness of the world. The Sun represents the Fools newfound joy and optimism which is needed for inner spiritual growth.

Now, he enjoys vibrant energy and enthusiasm. The Fool, like the naked babe pictured on the card, rides out joyously to face a new day. No challenge is too daunting. The Fool feels a radiant vitality. He becomes involved in grand undertakings as he draws to himself everything he needs. He is able to realize his greatness. The Fool knows that you do not know what pure enlightenment is unless you have been in the dark. The Fool is now in the light.

★ ★ ★

QUICK! JOT DOWN YOUR FIRST THOUGHTS ON THIS CARD.

THE SUN.

THE SUN

19

The Sun exemplifies beauty, radiance, abundance, and success. It represents abundant inner energy radiating through you. The Sun itself brings you strength and happiness. You will fulfill your own personal goals through the Sun's inspiration and energy and bring warmth into other people's lives. If you're in a difficult period, the Sun is peaking out to let you know everything will get better. Tap into your power and radiate and shine your authentic love on those you care about.

LOCATE THE FOLLOWING WORDS IN THE WORDSEARCH ON THE NEXT PAGE:

- ASSURANCE
- COURAGE
- ENERGY
- ENLIGHTENMENT
- GREATNESS
- HAPPINESS
- OPTIMISM
- POSITIVITY
- PROSPERITY
- RADIATE
- REWARDS
- SUCCESS
- VICTORY
- VITALITY
- WARMTH

THE SUN

- 19 -

```
B Z Z K I F W C V F P W P N K E V T C X
O C U H R R O U G T J A F X N R I C E P
M M M P G B G X J U K M N E J X K I S S
Y T I R E P S O R P Q K R W Q Q Z U V S
T M F S D R A W E R M G A C L U K B D E
T M L H S Q C O M E Y U I D G V C D K C
P M E O H O S U L E T A I D A R J C V C
A A A C U I O P O S I T I V I T Y T P U
T H P R N N X P S A C I M V R H E I K S
E O A H N A A C T S A S D Q Q B V B X A
L G A U E H R F S I E B Q L J Q A D Q J
E P I A M N B U R N M N W Q D J J S N R
U D Y J A C C M S I U I I A K S N S F Z
A H T Z E F C X U S P O S P P M T E F R
F S I O N O F B M C A Q G M P M Q N N V
U J L N I D R N B B V Z T Z S A G T D D
C G A I B F P U U K D F P O H A H A Z N
H S T T N E M N E T H G I L N E N E H Q
W M I M D F Y R O T C I V V A C S R U S
B A V C S Q W A R M T H N X W F A G B F
```

JUDGEMENT

- 20 -
ENLIGHTENMENT

The Fool has been reborn. With the Sun, his false, ego-self has been shed, allowing his radiant, true self to manifest. He has discovered that joy, not fear, is at life's center.

The Fool feels absolved. He forgives himself and others, knowing that his real self is pure and good. He may regret past mistakes, but he knows they were due to the ignorance of his true nature. He feels cleansed and refreshed, ready to start anew.

It is time for the Fool to make a deeper Judgement about his life. His own personal day of reckoning has arrived. Since he now sees himself truly, he can make the necessary decisions about the future. He can choose wisely which values to cherish, and which to discard.

The angel on this card is the Fool's Higher Self calling him to rise up and fulfill his promise. He discovers his true vocation - his reason for entering this life. Doubts and hesitations vanish, and he is ready to follow his dream.

★ ★ ★

QUICK! JOT DOWN YOUR FIRST THOUGHTS ON THIS CARD.

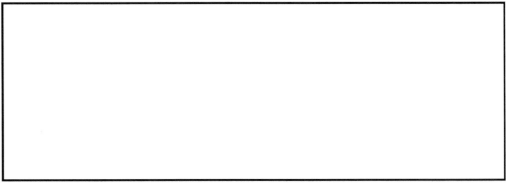

JUDGMENT.

JUDGEMENT

- 20 -

This card calls on you to rise up and embrace a higher level of consciousness. This is your spiritual awakening. If a decision needs to be made, unlike using the logic of Justice, blend intuition and intellect, trust your own judgment, and know that you are on the right path. It is telling you to reflect and evaluate your life and your actions and learn from past experiences by purging past regrets or guilt. You will be awakened by your own self-reflection, and any actions you take once you find yourself will change the course of your life.

LOCATE THE FOLLOWING WORDS IN THE WORDSEARCH ON THE NEXT PAGE:

- ABSOLUTION
- ACCEPTANCE
- CROSSROADS
- DESTINY
- FINALITY
- INNER CALLING
- JUDGEMENT
- LIFE-CHANGING CHOICE
- SUMMATION
- REBIRTH
- REGRETS
- REMORSE
- RENEWAL
- RESOLUTION
- SPIRITUAL AWAKENING

JUDGEMENT

- 20 -

```
M X N E R X E E C M V A E B Q A M O L U
T X M R L O E E A O V Z I H C X X C I G
E I J X K I E Q K W Q L S C Z P P H F N
R H X I F W C V F P W P E N R R K W E I
E V T K Q T R Z D D R P R R E E X G C N
G N A M W L P A U Z T M E K S N K C H E
R F O E U F X H O A J L B M O E H W A K
E J E I R P J V N P K R I X L W N N N A
T G I H T V N C I G A F R E U A O P G W
S H G C N U E O L Y Z H T W T L Z X I A
O B K W X I L I I A T M H W I C N A N L
W Q D J K J L O C T O I C V O I I G G A
J K F T U M C W S X A F L U N C L R C U
O G O V G T T F Z B F M M A P O P Y H T
W S I E S R O M E R A F M S N U P N O I
K H P Z C P H N E Z L M B U M I Q I I R
V P E B B B D R V A N V T O S B F T C I
C I M W R H S D A O R S S O R C I S E P
O G N I L L A C R E N N I L E C K E J S
I G V V G L J U D G E M E N T S F D Q D
```

THE WORLD

- 21 -

ENLIGHTENMENT

The Fool reenters the World, but this time with a more complete understanding. He has integrated all the disparate parts of himself and achieved wholeness. He has reached a new level of happiness and fulfillment. His journey has come to a successful end.

The Fool experiences life as full and meaningful. The future is filled with infinite promise. In line with his calling, he becomes actively involved in the world. He renders service by sharing his unique gifts and talents and finds that he prospers at whatever he attempts. Because he acts from inner certainty, the whole world conspires to see that his efforts are rewarded. His accomplishments are many.

So the Fool's Journey was not so foolish after all. Through perseverance and honesty, he reestablished the spontaneous courage that first impelled him on his search for Self, but now he is fully aware of his place in the world. This cycle is over, but, the Fool will never stop growing. Soon he will be ready to begin a new journey that will lead him to ever greater levels of understanding.

QUICK! JOT DOWN YOUR FIRST THOUGHTS ON THIS CARD.

THE WORLD.

THE WORLD

- 21 -

The World card represents a sense of wholeness, achievement, fulfillment, and completion. Everything has come full circle and you are reveling in the sense of closure and accomplishment of the intended goal when the journey began. Reflect on the journey, honor your achievements, and remember the spiritual lessons learned, and celebrate the success. Your journey has made you a stronger wiser person. If you have not reached the end, reflect back on the journey and revisit the obstacles and your experiences. This card asks you to complete your journey so you can clear space and welcome new opportunities.

LOCATE THE FOLLOWING WORDS IN THE WORDSEARCH ON THE NEXT PAGE:

- ACCOMPLISHMENT
- ACHIEVEMENT
- ATTAINMENT
- COMPLETION
- CYCLES
- FULFILLMENT
- INTEGRATION
- INVOLVEMENT
- NATURE
- PERFECTION
- RECOGNITION
- SELF-REALIZATION
- TRANSFORM
- TRAVEL
- WHOLENESS

THE WORLD

- 21 -

```
R F R H M G Z U U O C N Q T X A R Z Z D
G H C R G C X M P A O M P X C V L T D D
T Z B S O R B L E I L S P C E R U V E R
U I H J S W X I T M J I O O S W C H E B
S T R L K N F A J S M M G W J S M C P K
E E Z L I W R C S E P J C I F L O B B Z
L Z L K P G T E W L N S O J X G D K D C
F O J C E H N N I V L A T X N V I H H V
R V E T Y E M S E K O Q T I A P S O D I
E Q N N L C H R N M M R T U J E U S D A
A I D O G M J D O S L I F W R N L N D Q
L K H L E V A R T F O L F N T E L O L D
I W A N L Z B K O N S K I B D S L I K J
Z T T R X F T X V E O N H F T V E T B O
A C H I E V E M E N T Q A A L G R E O A
T T H M P G J U E U K S R R E U O L U A
I K S P F Z E H Z E F V C L T A F P R C
O Q D T J T T N E M N I A T T A L M F V
N G T N E M E V L O V N I M U L K O P I
L H F L V U P E R F E C T I O N M C F K
```

FIND THE DIFFERENCE

CAN YOU FIND THE DIFFERENCES
BETWEEN THESE TWO IMAGES?

THERE ARE 20 DIFFERENCES

DESIGN YOUR OWN

IS THE FOOL'S JOURNEY MISSING A STEP?
IF YOU COULD ADD A STEP WHAT WOULD IT BE? A LIBRARIAN?
AN ANGEL? A MYSTICAL CREATURE? DRAW YOUR IDEA HERE.

NUMEROLOGY
TAROT AND NUMEROLOGY CONNECTION

The study of numbers and their meanings is heavily weighted in Tarot. Understanding the numbers and their meaning can assist in interpreting the Minor Arcana cards.

It may help to think of the numbers 1-10 as a cycle. The Ace is the new beginning, there is growth through the mid-point, where things start to turn. In the end, not every ending is a happy, satisfied ending. The Ten of of Wands and Swords end on a downturn.

START

NUMEROLOGY

SUITS QUICK REFERENCE

NUMBER	KEYWORDS	CUPS, PENTACLES, SWORDS, WANDS
ACE	NEW CYCLES, INDIVIDUAL, SPARKS, DECISIONS	LOVE, MONEY, CHALLENGES, PROJECTS
TWO	CHOICES, BALANCE, PAIRINGS, PARTERNSHIPS	PARTNERSHIP, RESOURCE, DECISIONS, PLANNING
THREE	CREATING, GROWTH, CONNECTIONS, COLLABORATION	FRIENDS, COLLEAGUES, HEARTBREAK, TEAMWORK
FOUR	STABILITY, SECURITY, DEEP WORK, STRUCTURE, STAND STILL	STAGNATION, SECURITY, RECOVERY, LIFE
FIVE	CHALLENGE, CHANGE, CRISIS, INSTABILITY, CONFLICT	MEMORIES, LOSS, BULLIES, RIVALRY
SIX	EXPANSION, BALANCE, NEW NORMAL, HOPE	NOSTALIGIA, GENEROSITY, MOVING ON, ACCLAIM
SEVEN	INTERNAL WORK, REFLECTION, ASSESSMENT, SOLUTIONS	TEMPTATION, IMPATIENCE, TRICKERY, STANDING GROUND
EIGHT	INFINITY, SPEED, POWER, TRANSFORMATION	MOVING ON, MASTERY, TRAPPED, OPTIONS
NINE	CLIMAX, PEAK, SOLITUDE, MOMENTUM, NEAR COMPLETION	SATISFATION, ABUNDANCE, NIGHTMARES, BOUNDARIES
TEN	LETTING GO, COMPLETION, ENDINGS, ANOTHER BEGINNIING	CONTENT, INHERITANCE, ROCK BOTTOM, OVER BURDENED

MINOR ARCANA

ALSO KNOWN AS THE PIPS

The Minor Arcana is made up of 56 cards that represent everyday external circumstances or influences in your life. They assist us in making decisions and getting to know ourselves better.

The Minor Arcana comprises four suits, each containing ten numbered cards Ace thru Ten. As the numbers progress, the numbers represent a cycle of completion and lessons learned. The suits are:

Cups
Wands
Swords
Pentacles

Each suit also contains Court Cards which are considered masters of their suit, and more powerful than the numbered cards because they carry the wisdom and experience as they have already faced the lessons depicted in the numbered cards. The court cards are:

Page
Knight
Queen
King

NUMEROLOGY

TAROT AND NUMEROLOGY CONNECTION

1

2

3

4

5

6

7

8

9

10

- wholeness, end of cycle, completion

- duality, partnership, choice

- change, loss, instability

- collaboration, community, creativity

- intuition, magic, inspired action

- growth, near completion, alone

- foundation, structure, stability

- power, infinity, success

- new beginnings, individual, independence

- harmony, hope, balance

MATCHING

Keywords for each number 1-10 are above. See if you can match the words to the number on your own. Use your knowledge of the words, their representations in the world, or even the similarity with the shape of the number. Draw a line from the number to the keywords for that number.

FINISH THE PICTURE

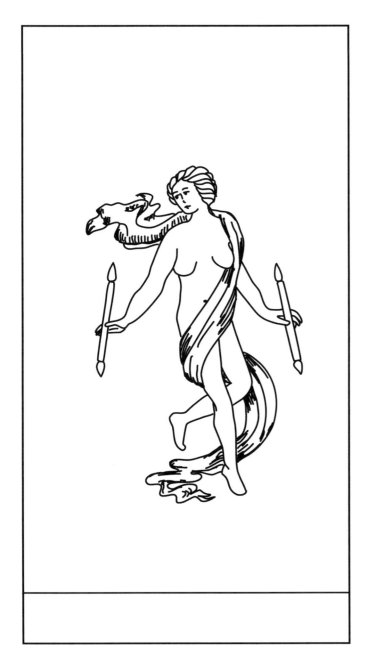

THE WORLD.

NUMEROLOGY TILES

REBUILD THE SENTENCE OR PHRASE

N_m_r_l_g_ _ll_ws ___ t_ _nd_rst_nd th_ p_w_r
l_rk_ng _n n_mb_rs _nd _nd_c_t_s th_t s_m_
th_ngs _n l_f_ m__ b_ _nt_rc_nn_ct_d. T_r_t
_nl_cks l_f_ w_th s_mb_ls, _ll_ws ___ t_
_nt_rpr_t ___rs_lf, ___r l_f_, _nd ___r f_t_r_, _nd
_mpr_v_ ___r _nt__t__n.

HINT: COMPLEMENTARY FRIENDS

_____

_____

_____

_____

_____

_____

_____

_____

MISSING VOWELS

Can you rebuild the phrase? Fill in the missing vowels to complete
the phrase.

SUITS AND ELEMENTS

	EARTH		AIR	FIRE	SWORDS		TAROT	WANDS
FIRE			EARTH			COINS	AIR	
CUPS	WANDS	AIR	COINS	TAROT	WATER			
EARTH	SWORDS					WANDS		COINS
	FIRE	WATER	SWORDS	COINS	EARTH			TAROT
	AIR		WATER		TAROT	EARTH		
	CUPS	WANDS						
SWORDS		FIRE			COINS		WANDS	
			WANDS				SWORDS	

HARD WORD SUDOKU

This version of Sudoku uses words instead of numbers. The words represent the four suits of the Minor Arcana, plus the four elements. The objective is to fill the grid with the words below so that each column, each row, and each of the four sub-grids contain all of the words.

CUPS	COINS	AIR
WANDS	WATER	EARTH
SWORDS	FIRE	TAROT

DESIGN YOUR OWN

THE DEATH CARD IS NOT ABOUT PHYSICAL DEALTH, BUT DEATH OF THE EGO. WOULD YOU REPRESENT THE DEATH IN A DIFFERENT WAY? DRAW YOUR INTERPRETATION BELOW.

SUIT OF CUPS

THE SUIT OF EMOTION

Cups rule the emotional realm which includes love and hate and everything in between. This includes intuition and spiritual feelings.

Think of the Suit of Cups as anything that moves your heart and emotions, not just feelings but visual arts and music as well.

Cups carry feminine energy and represent the element of Water.

Keywords for this suit are emotions, spirituality, artistic, creative, moods, love, feelings, relationships and connections.

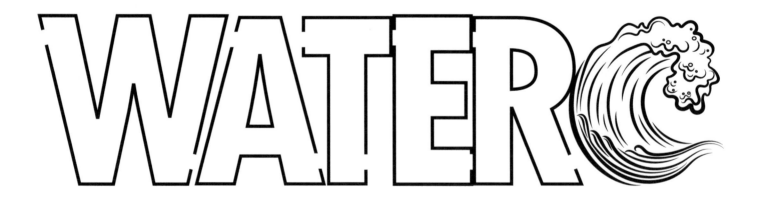

MINOR ARCANA
KEYWORDS OF THE SUIT

The Minor Arcana represents your everyday life ebb and flows. They represent daily activities, current situations or influences, as well as temporary situations that move through your life as you interact with others or yourself. Each suit has a ruling role or purpose.

REASON   WANDS

DESIRE   CUPS

CAREER   PENTACLES

EMOTION   SWORDS

MATCH THE FOLLOWING SUITS WITH THEIR KEYWORDS

Draw a line to match the suit with their keyword that describes the ruling role or purpose of the suit.

CUPS

KEYWORDS OF THE SUIT

IFELNSGE	
MISTOONE	
NIAOAIMNTIG	
LSORIPASNETIH	
LVEO	
SNCETNNIOOC	
WARET	
INTTIIONU	
NEIMFNEI	
NOMMSIATIRC	

WORD SCRAMBLE

Look carefully at the jumbled words and try unscrambling as many of the anagrams as you can into real words. The jumbled words have a theme of the positive expression for the Suit of Cups.

ELEMENTS

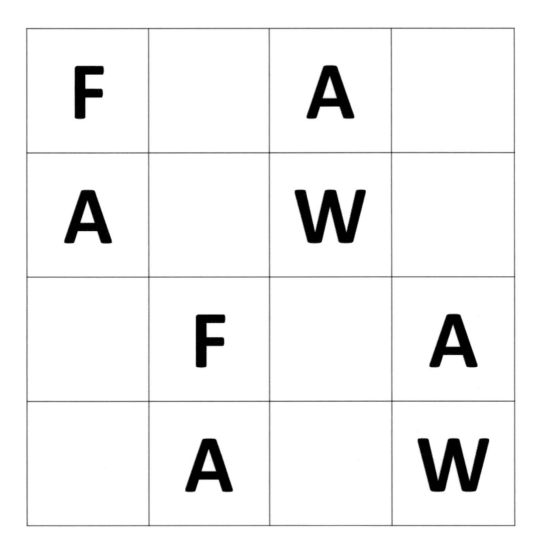

SUPER EASY SUDOKU

This simplified version of Sudoku uses letters instead of numbers. The letters represent the four elements which are represented by each Suit of the Minor Arcana. The objective is to fill the grid with digits so that each column, each row, and each of the four sub-grids contain all of the letters:

F=Fire E=Earth W=Water A=Air

TAROT TILES
REBUILD THE SENTENCE OR PHRASE

Th_ s__t _f C_ps _s c_nn_ct_d t_ __r _m_t__ns,
__r r_l_t__nsh_ps, _nd m_tt_rs _f th_ s__l.

HINT: SUIT OF EMOTION

_____

_____

_____

_____

_____

_____

_____

_____

_____

MISSING VOWELS
Can you rebuild the phrase? Fill in the missing vowels to complete the phrase.

HIDDEN OBJECT

CAN YOU FIND THE SNAKE IN THE PICTURE?

THE EMPRESS.

SUIT OF CUPS

ACE OF CUPS

		V		,						,						.				
X	U	K	R	,		X	U	K	R	,		X	U	K	R	.		L	R	C

B														O						
I	R	B	P	L	L	P	L	B	T		U	E		J	U	T	P	M	P	K	R

E																R		
R	Q	U	M	P	U	L	H	X		R	L	R	O	B	S		H	O	R

		N		P								.		
I	R	P	L	B		J	O	R	T	R	L	M	R	A	.

TWO OF CUPS

	B															
F	V	F	G	F	Y	H	M	Y	Q		F	H	I		Z	B

T				,		O								,		A		
I	W	N	T	I	,	H	Z	O	K	F	T	T	M	Z	Y	,	F	Y	S

R				C				E						
W	L	T	K	L	H	I		M	T		Y	L	L	S	L	S		M	Y

		P					S				
F	Y	R		K	F	W	I	Y	L	W	T	P	M	K

		G		.
L	Y	L	W	Q	R	.

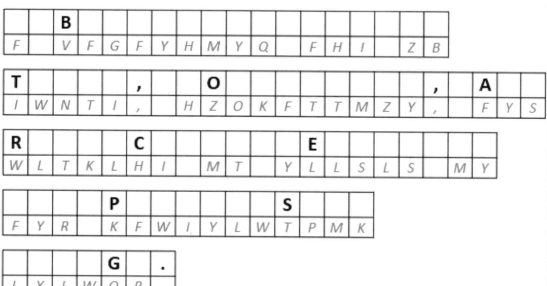

CRYPTOGRAM

Decode this short piece of encrypted text related to each card. Cryptograms can often be solved by frequency analysis, and by recognizing letter patterns in words, such as one letter words, which, in English, can only be "i" or "a". Hints and punctuation are given for each card.

SUIT OF CUPS

THREE OF CUPS

	O			V									
D	M	A		C	I	B	H		Y	M	A	P	S	D	M	A	O

T					.				N				
V	O	G	W	H	.		E	M	P	P	H	E	V		I	P	S

H					U		.					A	
C	I	B	H		Y	A	P	.		W	H		L	N	I	D	Y	A	N

			C								E	!
I	P	S		E	H	N	H	W	O	I	V	H	!

FOUR OF CUPS

B								R							
T	Z	G	D	B		J	W	B		A	C	G	D	B		Z	R		A	U	D

		E					G				.				
Y	J	V	D		Z	O	B		Q	J	V	D	.		A	J	M	D		J

	O					D					
O	Z	Z	M		J	G	Z	S	W	B		R	Z	G		A	U	D

	P										A	
Z	I	I	Z	G	A	S	W	C	A	C	D	Y		X	Z	S		J	G	D

		S				.
V	C	Y	Y	C	W	Q	.

CRYPTOGRAM

Decode this short piece of encrypted text related to each card. Cryptograms can often be solved by frequency analysis, and by recognizing letter patterns in words, such as one letter words, which, in English, can only be "i" or "a". Hints and punctuation are given for each card.

SUIT OF CUPS

FIVE OF CUPS

W								I		'		R					
X	U	O	A	U	O	W		V	A	'	F	W	O	N	W	O	A	,

	O					,			S					P			,
F	H	W	W	H	X	,		P	H	F	F		H	W		C	M	V	Z	,

	E									C						
J	O	O	P		V	A		M	Z	K		M	S	S	O	C	A		A	H

		V					.
G	H	Q	O		H	Z	.

SIX OF CUPS

			N					O		C								
F	U	O	B	M	M	U	O	Q		Q	B		O	C	Z	W	T	W	Z	X	U

W					,		Y								,
A	B	M	T	U	F	,		K	W	L	G	D	Y	W	M	U	J	J	,

				A						
L	M	T		L		O	L	F	U	D	F	U	U

				E	.					M		
L	Q	Q	Z	Q	Y	T	U	.		C	L	P	U		J	B	R	U

F			!
D	Y	M	!

CRYPTOGRAM

Decode this short piece of encrypted text related to each card. Cryptograms can often be solved by frequency analysis, and by recognizing letter patterns in words, such as one letter words, which, in English, can only be "i" or "a". Hints and punctuation are given for each card.

SUIT OF CUPS

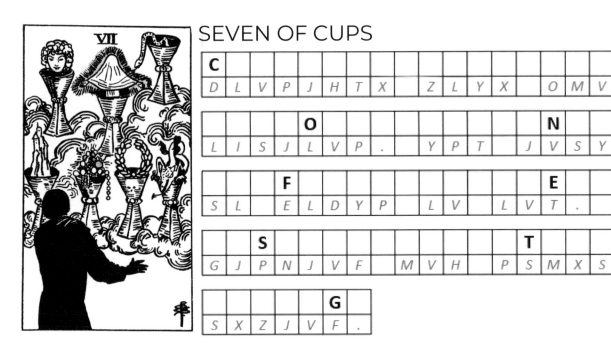

SEVEN OF CUPS

C																Y
D	L	V	P	J	H	T	X		Z	L	Y	X		O	M	V	Z

			O									N					
L	I	S	J	L	V	P	.		Y	P	T		J	V	S	Y	J	S	J	L	V

		F										E					
S	L		E	L	D	Y	P		L	V		L	V	T	.		P	S	L	I

			S								T					
G	J	P	N	J	V	F		M	V	H		P	S	M	X	S

				G			
S	X	Z	J	V	F	.

EIGHT OF CUPS

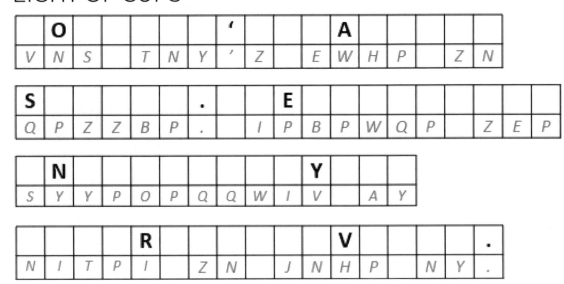

	O						'				A					
V	N	S		T	N	Y	'	Z		E	W	H	P		Z	N

S					.			E								
Q	P	Z	Z	B	P	.		I	P	B	P	W	Q	P		Z	E	P

	N							Y					
S	Y	Y	P	O	P	Q	Q	W	I	V		A	Y

			R						V				.
N	I	T	P	I		Z	N		J	N	H	P		N	Y	.

CRYPTOGRAM

Decode this short piece of encrypted text related to each card. Cryptograms can often be solved by frequency analysis, and by recognizing letter patterns in words, such as one letter words, which, in English, can only be "i" or "a". Hints and punctuation are given for each card.

SUIT OF CUPS

NINE OF CUPS

		S						**E**				
S	L	G	I	H	P	G	V	P	L	N	I	F	N

G										**Y**			
O	A	I	H	L	V	M	Q	U	P	H	D	X	E	M	A

R						.			'			**W**				
A	L	U	I	A	N	G	.	X	E	M	'	B	L	U	E	A	C	L	N

			.		**A**				**I**		.
D	I	A	N	.	G	I	B	E	A	P	H	.

TEN OF CUPS

	O		'				**A**					**T**			
I	A	T	'	C	D	E	D	F	W	V	D	S	H	E	T	D

E												**L**					.
D	Y	A	H	U	A	G	F	N	Q	T	N	Q	U	N	N	Y	D	G	H	.

W			'			**X**	**?**
R	V	F	H	'	P	G	D	J	H	?

CRYPTOGRAM

Decode this short piece of encrypted text related to each card. Cryptograms can often be solved by frequency analysis, and by recognizing letter patterns in words, such as one letter words, which, in English, can only be "i" or "a". Hints and punctuation are given for each card.

SUIT OF CUPS

PAGE of CUPS.

PAGE OF CUPS

T										E						
A	D	B	E	B		J	E	B		X	B	R	R	J	Z	B	R

			M					X						
S	E	K	X		I	L	B	Y	N	B	O	A	B	G

		U									F					O		
R	K	I	E	O	B	R		K	E		S	E	K	X		U	K	I	E

	W										N	.
K	V	L		T	L	A	I	T	A	T	K	L	.

KNIGHT OF CUPS

			R								.							E	
X	I	Q		O	K	J	P	U	X	H	B	.		L	Q		K	D	Q	U

			X										
X	K		Q	A	D	F	K	O	H	U	E		X	I	Q

B							L			D					
L	Q	P	N	X	H	W	N	F		H	R	Q	P	M		H	U

	U										F				
C	K	N	O		I	Q	P	R		P	U	R		W	K	F	F	K	Y

O				S				.
C	K	N	O		D	P	M	M	H	K	U	.

KNIGHT of CUPS.

CRYPTOGRAM

Decode this short piece of encrypted text related to each card. Cryptograms can often be solved by frequency analysis, and by recognizing letter patterns in words, such as one letter words, which, in English, can only be "i" or "a". Hints and punctuation are given for each card.

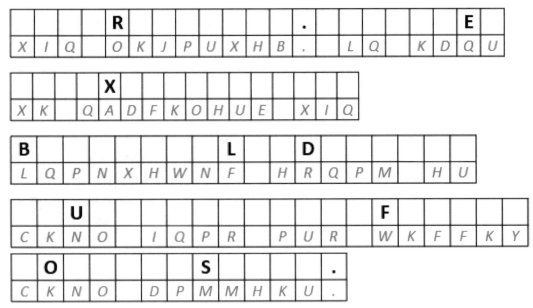

SUIT OF CUPS

QUEEN OF CUPS

QUEEN of CUPS.

	O						S							.			E			
H	I	K		Y	X	V		C	N	X	I	R	A	.		Q	V	Y	F	

			H							A		,					T
D	B	N	L		H	I	K	X		L	V	Y	X	N	,	N	X	K	C	N

			I												Y
H	I	K	X		B	R	N	K	B	N	B	I	R		Y	R	F	T	Y	H

					N				U			
Y	N	N	V	R	N	B	I	R		N	I		H	I	K	X

F								M					.
M	V	V	Q	B	R	A	C		Y	R	F		V	S	I	N	B	I	R	C	.

KING OF CUPS

					R							G
A	R	K		W	K	L	U	K	E		V	D	A	R		L		G	D	Z

H				.						U		
R	K	L	E	A	.		T	Y	O		M	L	S		O	B	K

L								O			E			
W	Y	Z	D	M		L	S	U		Z	Y	L	W		B	K	A	A	D	S	Z

W					K						
V	R	D	W	K		H	L	P	D	S	Z		B	O	E	K

			S					A					
Y	A	R	K	E	B		L	E	K		A	L	P	K	S		M	L	E	K

	F	.
Y	X	.

KING of CUPS.

CRYPTOGRAM

Decode this short piece of encrypted text related to each card. Cryptograms can often be solved by frequency analysis, and by recognizing letter patterns in words, such as one letter words, which, in English, can only be "i" or "a". Hints and punctuation are given for each card.

SUITS AND ELEMENTS

TAROT	AIR	CUPS		WANDS	WATER		FIRE	COINS
	FIRE		CUPS	COINS	SWORDS	WANDS	AIR	
	SWORDS	WANDS		TAROT			CUPS	WATER
	WANDS	TAROT		FIRE		WATER		
AIR		COINS	SWORDS			CUPS	TAROT	
SWORDS	EARTH	FIRE	TAROT	WATER			COINS	
WATER			COINS			FIRE		
FIRE	CUPS	EARTH		SWORDS	TAROT	COINS	WATER	
WANDS		AIR	WATER			TAROT		SWORDS

EASY WORD SUDOKU

This version of Sudoku uses words instead of numbers. The words represent the four suits of the Minor Arcana, plus the four elements. The objective is to fill the grid with the words below so that each column, each row, and each of the four sub-grids contain all of the words.

CUPS	COINS	AIR
WANDS	WATER	EARTH
SWORDS	FIRE	TAROT

DESIGN YOUR OWN

MANY DECKS CARRY A THEME: ANIMALS, FAIRIES, WITCHES, POP CULTURE AND MORE. WHAT WOULD YOUR IDEAL THEME BE? DRAW THE FOOL CARD IN YOUR FAVORITE THEME.

SUIT OF PENTACLES

THE SUIT OF EARTHLY MATTER

Pentacles can sometimes be referred to as coins or discs, and represent any worldly thing made of matter and acts of work.

They can be thought of as any tangible thing, including the body, or anything that represents wealth or stability such as a career.

The Suit of Pentacles represents the element of Earth, and carries feminine energy.

Keywords for this suit are health, finances, work, worldly matters, security and prosperity.

MINOR ARCANA

KEYWORDS OF THE SUIT

The Minor Arcana represents your everyday life ebb and flows. They represent daily activities, current situations or influences, as well as temporary situations that move through your life as you interact with others or yourself. Each suit has a ruling role or purpose.

INTELLECT	CUPS
WEALTH	WANDS
PASSION	PENTACLES
LOVE	SWORDS

MATCH THE FOLLOWING SUITS WITH THEIR KEYWORDS

Draw a line to match the suit with their keyword that describes the ruling role ourpose of the suit.

PENTACLES

KEYWORDS OF THE SUIT

NAFCNESI	
REEACR	
SOPSISSESON	
GINTLEAB	
EATLWH	
AELHHT	
IEIVYCRATT	
ERTHA	
FSIEANTMIANOT	
PROSTIPYRE	

WORD SCRAMBLE

Look carefully at the jumbled words and try unscrambling as many of the anagrams as you can into real words. The jumbled words have a theme of the positive expression for the Suit of Pentacles.

SUITS

W		C	
C		S	
	W		C
	C		S

SUPER EASY SUDOKU

This simplified version of Sudoku uses letters instead of numbers. The letters represent the four suits of the Minor Arcana. The objective is to fill the grid with digits so that each column, each row, and each of the four sub-grids contain all of the letters:

P=PENTACLES S=SWORDS W=WANDS C=CUPS

TAROT TILES

REBUILD THE SENTENCE OR PHRASE

Th_ P_nt_cl_s s__t p_rt__ns t_ th_ngs _n th_
m_t_r__l _nd ph_s_c_l w_rld s_ch _s w__lth _nd
m_n__ b_t _ls_ t_ s_cc_ss _nd pr_sp_r_t_ s_ch _s
c_r__r s_cc_ss, f_m_l_, b_d_, _nd h__lth m_tt_rs.

HINT: SUIT OF SUCCESS

_____

_____

_____

_____

_____

_____

_____

_____

_____

MISSING VOWELS

Can you rebuild the phrase? Fill in the missing vowels to complete the phrase.

FIND THE DIFFERENCE

CAN YOU FIND THE DIFFERENCES
BETWEEN THESE TWO IMAGES?

THERE ARE 14 DIFFERENCES

SUIT OF PENTACLES

ACE OF PENTACLES

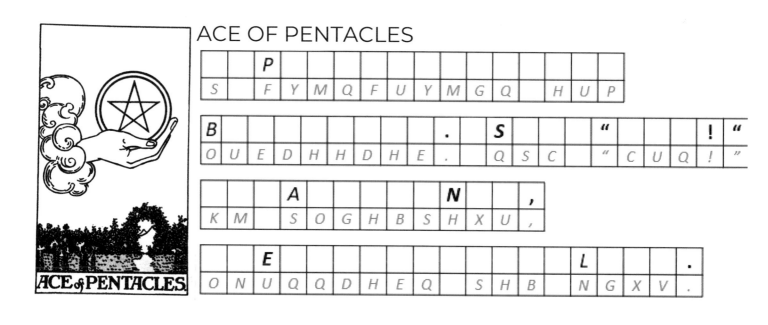

		P													
S		F	Y	M	Q	F	U	Y	M	G	Q		H	U	P

B							.		S			"			!	"
O	U	E	D	H	H	D	H	E	.		Q	S	C	"	C	U	Q	!	"

			A				N			,
K	M		S	O	G	H	B	S	H	X	U	,

		E								L				.
O	N	U	Q	Q	D	H	E	Q		S	H	B		N	G	X	V	.

TWO OF PENTACLES

			A			B												
O	H	E		P	N	V		U	P	B	P	G	F	C	G	K		O	H	E	N

			G											.
H	U	B	C	K	P	Z	C	H	G	T		Q	V	B	B	.

	O							P								.
A	H	F	E	T		H	G		Y	N	C	H	N	C	Z	C	V	T	.

CRYPTOGRAM

Decode this short piece of encrypted text related to each card. Cryptograms can often be solved by frequency analysis, and by recognizing letter patterns in words, such as one letter words, which, in English, can only be "i" or "a". Hints and punctuation are given for each card.

SUIT OF PENTACLES

THREE OF PENTACLES

T															
O	H	R	C	A	V	D	S		V	T	H	D		O	M	H

I				V						.					
F	W	J	F	T	F	J	B	R	K	.		C	R	S	H

S					Y									R	
U	B	D	H		P	V	B	D		Q	R	D	O	W	H	D	U

			E						.	
R	D	H		H	Y	B	R	K	U	.

FOUR OF PENTACLES

S								D					'	
L	N	H	P	U	S	D	V	C	B	N	L	Z	'	D

	L							F							
K	E	T	K	V	L		H	B	A	N		R	U	B	A		D	Q	N

					W					.				E	
A	K	D	N	U	S	K	E		T	B	U	E	C	.		E	B	B	L	N	Z

	O				P	.
V	B	P	U		X	U	S	G	.

CRYPTOGRAM

Decode this short piece of encrypted text related to each card. Cryptograms can often be solved by frequency analysis, and by recognizing letter patterns in words, such as one letter words, which, in English, can only be "i" or "a". Hints and punctuation are given for each card.

SUIT OF PENTACLES

FIVE OF PENTACLES

							E			O		
B	R		S	Z	M	G	L	H	P	L	W	Z	Z	H

A					,		Y							
L	X	Z	M	Q	O	,	S	Z	M	I	L	Q	R	B	Q	O

			.			'		F				
D	P	W	F	.	O	Z	Q	'	G	R	Z	I	M	V	Z	Q

								L				.
J	D	L	G	S	Z	M	L	X	P	W	L	I	H	B	Q	T	.

SIX OF PENTACLES

D			'						F						
C	G	Z	'	Y	R	S	Q	T	L	Q	F	C	Y	G	R	S

G								I					
D	S	Z	S	L	G	W	K	H	F	Y	I	Q	N	N	B	G	W

			.		V						T	
I	Q	A	S	.	D	F	A	F	Z	D	I	Q	K	F	Y	K

			R					.	
G	H	Z	L	S	H	Q	L	C	K	.

CRYPTOGRAM

Decode this short piece of encrypted text related to each card. Cryptograms can often be solved by frequency analysis, and by recognizing letter patterns in words, such as one letter words, which, in English, can only be "i" or "a". Hints and punctuation are given for each card.

SUIT OF PENTACLES

SEVEN OF PENTACLES

					R													**O**	
X	J	Q	E	D	P	M	M	D	A		C	M	B	E		U	M	P	

			F						.						
D	W	K	U	I	D	I	P	K	.		P	K	V	Q	R	E

P																
X	Q	D	R	K	E	D		D	M		P	K	Q	X		D	W	K

		E											
H	K	E	K	U	R	D	A		M	U		L	M	I	P

			L				.
B	M	P	Z		J	Q	D	K	P	.

EIGHT OF PENTACLES

	I					**R**			**L**					.
X	C	G	W		U	R	P	T		F	D	J	J	C	G	Y	.

H													
M	R	G	Z		U	R	P	T		E	D	O	M		D	G	W

	O		'		**G**						.
W	R	G	'	O		Y	C	Q	Z		P	E	.

CRYPTOGRAM

Decode this short piece of encrypted text related to each card. Cryptograms can often be solved by frequency analysis, and by recognizing letter patterns in words, such as one letter words, which, in English, can only be "i" or "a". Hints and punctuation are given for each card.

SUIT OF PENTACLES

NINE OF PENTACLES

			'		E							C			
S	Z	Y	'	R	V		G	V	T	H	K	V	Q		

F																		
D	Y	X	D	N	X	X	A	V	J	E		T	J	Q		N	E	

					L									.	
D	V	V	X	C		X	Y	L	Y	G	N	Z	Y	C	.

		J								U					
V	J	I	Z	S		E	K	V		D	G	Y	N	E	C	Z	D

		O					B			.
S	Z	Y	G		X	T	P	Z	G	.

TEN OF PENTACLES

							R						.		.		U
Q	E	M		N	B	Y	X		B	Z	Z	C	Y	X	L	.		Q	E	M

			S										
B	Z	X		R	M	Z	Z	E	M	W	L	X	L		J	Q

	B						.					E			
B	J	M	W	L	B	W	O	X	.		R	N	B	Z	X		A	C	F	N

	O						L		.
F	N	E	R	X		Q	E	M		D	E	Y	X	.

CRYPTOGRAM

Decode this short piece of encrypted text related to each card. Cryptograms can often be solved by frequency analysis, and by recognizing letter patterns in words, such as one letter words, which, in English, can only be "i" or "a". Hints and punctuation are given for each card.

SUIT OF PENTACLES

PAGE of PENTACLES.

PAGE OF PENTACLES

			S													
I	Z	A	W	W	I	E	A	R	T	W	V	I	U	B	G	B	V	N

			P										.				E
I	C	H	Y	P	R	W	Y	A	P	B	V	N	.	I	P	A

			C											A			W
N	R	Q	L	R	C	W	B	H	A	P	B	C	E	I	C	A	J

		T	?
Y	I	V	M	?

KNIGHT OF PENTACLES

S		W							E							
P	T	I	G	F	S	V	P	Y	O	F	V	J	G	B	S	P

			R			.			'		A				
Y	A	O	H	F	L	O	.	B	Y	'	P	F	T	I	S	D

G													
D	F	Q	O	Y	A	F	Y	L	F	S	S	I	Y	U	O

	U				.
H	K	P	A	O	V	.

KNIGHT of PENTACLES.

CRYPTOGRAM

Decode this short piece of encrypted text related to each card. Cryptograms can often be solved by frequency analysis, and by recognizing letter patterns in words, such as one letter words, which, in English, can only be "i" or "a". Hints and punctuation are given for each card.

SUIT OF PENTACLES

QUEEN OF PENTACLES

Y												A		:
V	U	M	Y	P	A	K	U	O	H	P	I	I	:	

W			,				I		,
Z	U	S	F	,	T	P	G	O	I	V	,

		D								,
O	A	K	Q	D	Q	A	K	Q	A	Y	Q	,

		B								
P	J	M	A	K	P	A	Y	Q	P	A	K

S						.			C			O
W	Q	Y	M	S	O	H	V	.	T	U	Y	M	W	U	A

						.
J	P	I	P	A	Y	Q	.

KING OF PENTACLES

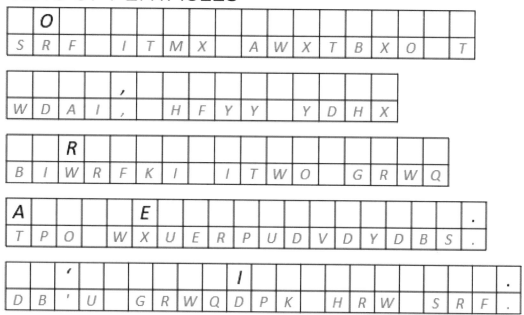

	O											
S	R	F	I	T	M	X	A	W	X	T	B	X	O	T

			,							
W	D	A	I	,	H	F	Y	Y	Y	D	H	X

		R								
B	I	W	R	F	K	I	I	T	W	O	G	R	W	Q

A				E								.
T	P	O	W	X	U	E	R	P	U	D	V	D	Y	D	B	S	.

		'					I				.
D	B	'	U	G	R	W	Q	D	P	K	H	R	W	S	R	F	.

CRYPTOGRAM

Decode this short piece of encrypted text related to each card. Cryptograms can often be solved by frequency analysis, and by recognizing letter patterns in words, such as one letter words, which, in English, can only be "i" or "a". Hints and punctuation are given for each card.

SUITS AND ELEMENTS

FIRE	COINS			EARTH	SWORDS	CUPS	AIR	TAROT
SWORDS	TAROT	CUPS	COINS	WANDS	AIR	WATER	FIRE	
		WATER	TAROT	FIRE	CUPS	COINS		WANDS
WANDS			AIR				WATER	
		FIRE		SWORDS	EARTH		TAROT	
	CUPS	TAROT		WATER	WANDS	AIR		SWORDS
CUPS				AIR			WANDS	FIRE
TAROT	FIRE	SWORDS		CUPS	WATER	EARTH	COINS	
			SWORDS	COINS	FIRE			

EASY WORD SUDOKU

This version of Sudoku uses words instead of numbers. The words represent the four suits of the Minor Arcana, plus the four elements. The objective is to fill the grid with the words below so that each column, each row, and each of the four sub-grids contain all of the words.

CUPS	COINS	AIR
WANDS	WATER	EARTH
SWORDS	FIRE	TAROT

FINISH THE PICTURE

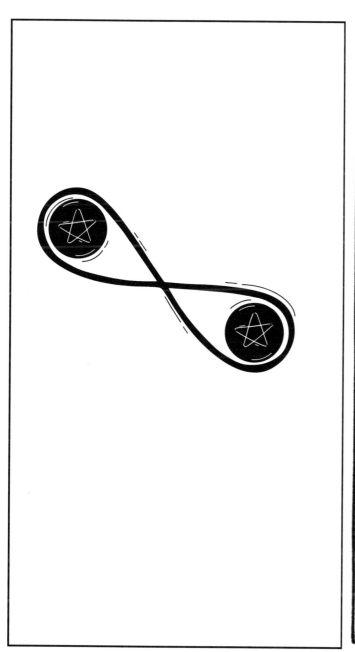

SUIT OF SWORDS

THE SUIT OF INTELLECT

Swords represent the intellectual realm such as thought, logic, and reason. Think of a sword aligning with your head and the many functions of your mind such as sight, sound, thought, etc.

Swords carry masculine energy and are associated with the element of Air.

Keywords for this suit are thoughts, ideas, intellect, communication, attitudes and spoken words.

MINOR ARCANA

KEYWORDS OF THE SUIT

The Minor Arcana represents your everyday life ebb and flows. They represent daily activities, current situations or influences, as well as temporary situations that move through your life as you interact with others or yourself. Each suit has a ruling role or purpose.

ACTION   SWORDS

CLARITY   WANDS

GROUNDING   CUPS

FEELINGS   PENTACLES

MATCH THE FOLLOWING SUITS WITH THEIR KEYWORDS

Draw a line to match the suit with their keyword that describes the ruling role or purpose of the suit.

SWORDS

KEYWORDS OF THE SUIT

UTGOHHTS	
ORSWD	
CTNAOSI	
ESDIA	
SDOEIINCS	
WEROP	
AENTML	
LIEFBE	
ATIETDUT	
OITIBANM	

WORD SCRAMBLE

Look carefully at the jumbled words and try unscrambling as many of the anagrams as you can into real words. The jumbled words have a theme of the positive expression for the Suit of Swords.

ELEMENTS

A	E		
W		E	
	W		F
		W	E

SUPER EASY SUDOKU

This simplified version of Sudoku uses letters instead of numbers. The letters represent the four elements which are represented by each Suit of the Minor Arcana. The objective is to fill the grid with digits so that each column, each row, and each of the four sub-grids contain all of the letters:

F=Fire E=Earth W=Water A=Air

TAROT TILES

REBUILD THE SENTENCE OR PHRASE

Th_ Sw_rds s__t h_lps ___ pr_p_r_ f_r l_f_'s
gr__t_st ch_ll_ng_s, _nd r_m_nd ___ _f ___r _wn
kn_wl_dg_ _nd str_ngth.

HINT: SUIT OF LOGIC

_____

_____

_____

_____

_____

_____

_____

_____

_____

MISSING VOWELS

Can you rebuild the phrase? Fill in the missing vowels to complete
the phrase.

FIND THE DIFFERENCE

CAN YOU FIND THE DIFFERENCES
BETWEEN THESE TWO REVERSED IMAGES?

THERE ARE 11 DIFFERENCES

SUIT OF SWORDS

ACE of SWORDS.

ACE OF SWORDS

A				B										
N		A	H	F		X	H	T	Z	A	A	Z	A	T		Q	I

								G		
Z	V	H	N		Z	L		X	H	Z	A	T

P						E	.						O		
C	I	H	L	H	A	B	H	V	.		B	I	Y	L	B		D	Q	Y	I

I										U					
Z	A	B	Y	Z	B	Z	Q	A		B	Q		T	Y	Z	V	H		D	Q	Y

		R					.
G	Q	I	F	N	I	V	.

TWO OF SWORDS

D																
S	H	W	F	Q	F	T	Y	Q		Y	H	H	S		O	T

		M				.					'			E
I	H		E	V	S	H	.		S	T	Y	'	O		I	H

	A				Z						
A	V	C	V	K	G	P	H	S		I	G

N								.			R			
F	Y	S	H	W	F	Q	F	T	Y	.		O	C	D	Q	O

O				U		.
G	T	D	C		M	D	O	.

CRYPTOGRAM

Decode this short piece of encrypted text related to each card. Cryptograms can often be solved by frequency analysis, and by recognizing letter patterns in words, such as one letter words, which, in English, can only be "i" or "a". Hints and punctuation are given for each card.

SUIT OF SWORDS

THREE OF SWORDS

B										E							
J	S	F	W	V		H	R	G	S	Z	V	C	T		T	R	S

	H																N
W	K	F	B	X	V		N	K	S	R	G	X	K		O	F	M	B

				T				.			C					
R	S		N	S	G	N	K	Z	.		F	W	W	V	O	N

			R					O					.
M	B		R	S	Y	V	S		N	R		K	V	F	C	.

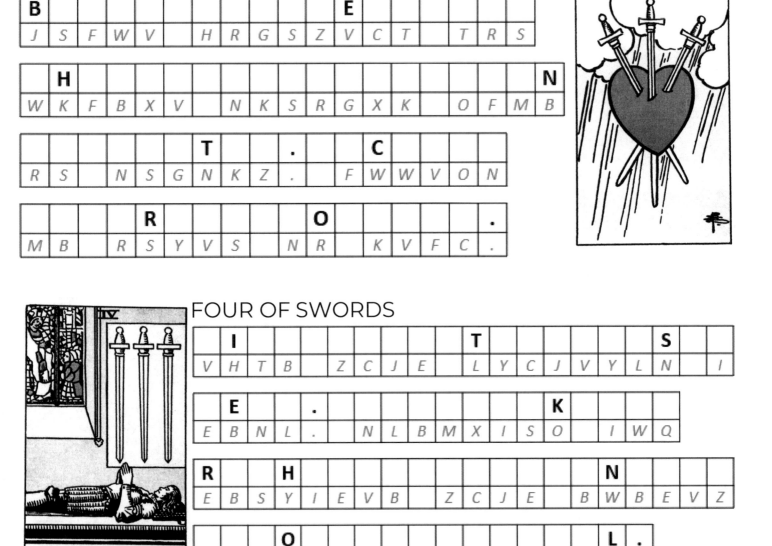

FOUR OF SWORDS

	I							T						S		
V	H	T	B		Z	C	J	E		L	Y	C	J	V	Y	L	N		I

	E		.								K			
E	B	N	L	.		N	L	B	M	X	I	S	O		I	W	Q

R		H										N		
E	B	S	Y	I	E	V	B		Z	C	J	E		B	W	B	E	V	Z

		O								L	.
H	W		C	E	Q	B	E		L	C		Y	B	I	U	.

CRYPTOGRAM

Decode this short piece of encrypted text related to each card. Cryptograms can often be solved by frequency analysis, and by recognizing letter patterns in words, such as one letter words, which, in English, can only be "i" or "a". Hints and punctuation are given for each card.

SUIT OF SWORDS

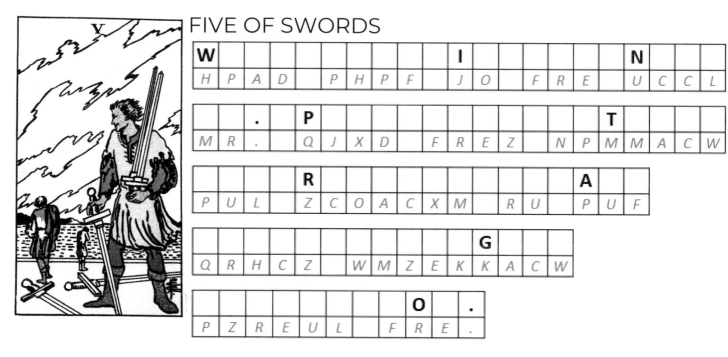

FIVE OF SWORDS

W									I						N		
H	P	A	D		P	H	P	F		J	O		F	R	E	U	C	C	L

			.		P										T		
M	R	.		Q	J	X	D		F	R	E	Z		N	P	M	M	A	C	W

				R									A		
P	U	L		Z	C	O	A	C	X	M		R	U		P	U	F

									G		
Q	R	H	C	Z		W	M	Z	E	K	K	A	C	W

							O		.
P	Z	R	E	U	L		F	R	E	.

SIX OF SWORDS

									A						.			
U	F	F	Z		J	E	B	T	C	A		G	W	F	G	Q	.		S	W	F

W					S			H					O		.
K	E	V	H	S		T	H		R	F	W	T	C	Q		M	E	L	.

	K			E				I				
J	G	U	F		Z	F	G	Y	F		K	T	S	W		S	W	F

P							R						
Z	G	H	S		G	C	Q		S	V	L	H	S		S	W	F

F						.
D	L	S	L	V	F	.

CRYPTOGRAM

Decode this short piece of encrypted text related to each card. Cryptograms can often be solved by frequency analysis, and by recognizing letter patterns in words, such as one letter words, which, in English, can only be "i" or "a". Hints and punctuation are given for each card.

SUIT OF SWORDS

SEVEN OF SWORDS

S								C	X		U	J	C	K	L
X	M	Q	J	M	K	J		C	X		U	J	C	K	L

		E							D							.
X	K	J	R	W	V		M	E		H	J	T	J	D	B	C	F	J	.

	R				O				G							
R	E	J		V	M	S		C	L	K	M	E	C	K	L		B	N	J

			N		?
X	C	L	K	X	?

EIGHT OF SWORDS

F								P				?				
B	Y	Y	P	R	J	E		H	N	F	M	M	Y	Z	?		S	Q	V

A		E					T				.			O	
F	N	Y		J	Q	H		T	H	V	U	W	.		S	Q	V

M												R			
X	R	E	I	H		K	Y		R	J		S	Q	V	N		Q	A	J

W			.
A	F	S	.

CRYPTOGRAM

Decode this short piece of encrypted text related to each card. Cryptograms can often be solved by frequency analysis, and by recognizing letter patterns in words, such as one letter words, which, in English, can only be "i" or "a". Hints and punctuation are given for each card.

SUIT OF SWORDS

NINE OF SWORDS

			Y		**R**		**X**					
N	S	V	V	H	S	V	E	C	G	K	F	X	H	K	R

	E											
T	F	F	Q	K	C	W	H	S	J	J	Q	E	X

N				**.**		**I**				**W**		
C	K	W	U	X	.	Y	K	C	O	E	N	E	H	X	S

	H					**T**	**.**
I	U	E	C	C	F	M	K	X	.

TEN OF SWORDS

G				**V**		**.**						**W**		**,**
I	U	K	O	Q	J	O	T	.	V	B	U	C	E	Q	Z	H	,

A						**R**						
U	Y	Y	O	L	B	B	N	O	T	O	V	S	D	B	U	H	E

				T								**S**	
T	O	G	D	O	Y	B	Q	H	B	N	O	D	O	V	V	Q	H	V

L			**E**		**.**
D	O	U	T	H	O	E	.

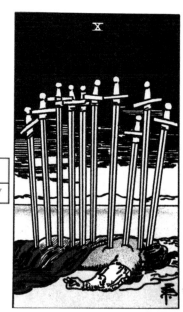

CRYPTOGRAM

Decode this short piece of encrypted text related to each card. Cryptograms can often be solved by frequency analysis, and by recognizing letter patterns in words, such as one letter words, which, in English, can only be "i" or "a". Hints and punctuation are given for each card.

SUIT OF SWORDS

PAGE OF SWORDS

F					W												
G	U	Y	N	E		S	Y	J		Z	T	Y	R	N		R	S	T

A			E		P									I			.
R		S	Y	J		F	Y	U	N	F	Y	Q	I	Z	L	Y	.

L								H				
H	Z	N	I	Y	S		I	K		J	E	R	I

S									R					
N	M	U	U	K	M	S	T	N		X	K	M		U	Z	V	E	I

	O		.
S	K	J	.

PAGE of SWORDS.

KNIGHT OF SWORDS

	T	'				E			A					
Z	M	'	V		M	Z	T	X		M	H		L	E	M	!		P	H	R

		N				O				.		D		
E	L	U	U	H	M		L	D	H	Z	F		Z	M	.		F	X	L	W

	I					S						.
S	Z	M	Q		P	H	R	A		V	Z	M	R	L	M	Z	H	U	.

KNIGHT of SWORDS.

CRYPTOGRAM

Decode this short piece of encrypted text related to each card. Cryptograms can often be solved by frequency analysis, and by recognizing letter patterns in words, such as one letter words, which, in English, can only be "i" or "a". Hints and punctuation are given for each card.

SUIT OF SWORDS

QUEEN OF SWORDS

S						O				U				.
A	D	C	E	P		I	V	R	G		Z	G	R	Z	K	.

C						I											
W	V	O	O	R	H	W	Y	E	Z	C		W	Q	C	E	G	Q	I

			L					E						
E	H	T		Q	C	E	X	C		C	O	V	Z	Y	V	H	A

		T		F			.
V	R	Z		V	N		Y	Z	.

KING OF SWORDS

Y					'			G					I	
U	P	H		W	T	W	I	'	O		E	K	O		O	S	T	Y

	A						T							.
A	F	Q		L	U		Y	T	O	O	T	I	E		F	Q	P	H	I	W	.

U						C								
H	Y	K		U	P	H	Q		Z	P	G	G	H	I	T	Z	F	O	T	P	I

		L						O			
Y	X	T	B	B	Y		F	I	W		B	P	E	T	Z		O	P

		D						
B	K	F	W		F	I	W		Z	B	K	F	Q		H	C

		N					.
Z	P	I	A	H	Y	T	P	I	.

CRYPTOGRAM

Decode this short piece of encrypted text related to each card. Cryptograms can often be solved by frequency analysis, and by recognizing letter patterns in words, such as one letter words, which, in English, can only be "i" or "a". Hints and punctuation are given for each card.

SUITS AND ELEMENTS

	CUPS				SWORDS			TAROT
SWORDS			COINS	EARTH	AIR		FIRE	WANDS
EARTH	AIR	WANDS	CUPS		TAROT		COINS	
CUPS	FIRE		SWORDS	WANDS		TAROT	EARTH	AIR
		AIR	FIRE	CUPS			WANDS	COINS
WATER	WANDS	EARTH	AIR		COINS	FIRE		
WANDS			WATER					EARTH
	EARTH			COINS	CUPS	WANDS		FIRE
FIRE	WATER		EARTH		WANDS	COINS		CUPS

INTERMEDIATE WORD SUDOKU

This version of Sudoku uses words instead of numbers. The words represent the four suits of the Minor Arcana, plus the four elements. The objective is to fill the grid with the words below so that each column, each row, and each of the four sub-grids contain all of the words.

CUPS   COINS   AIR
WANDS   WATER   EARTH
SWORDS   FIRE   TAROT

FINISH THE PICTURE

ACE of WANDS.

SUIT OF WANDS

THE SUIT OF PASSION

Wands are sometimes called rods or staffs. They represent passion, desire, and creative force.

This suit is responsible for sparking a light, building enthusiasm, and maintaining energy, much like our Sacral Chakra.

Wands carry a masculine energy and represent the element of Fire.

Keywords for this suit include passion, energy, enthusiasm, action, movement, self expression, creativity, fire and sexuality.

MINOR ARCANA

KEYWORDS OF THE SUIT

The Minor Arcana represents your everyday life ebb and flows. They represent daily activities, current situations or influences, as well as temporary situations that move through your life as you interact with others or yourself. Each suit has a ruling element.

FIRE	PENTACLES
WATER	SWORDS
AIR	CUPS
EARTH	WANDS

MATCH THE FOLLOWING SUITS WITH THEIR KEYWORDS

Draw a line to match the suit with their keyword that describes the ruling element of the suit.

WANDS

KEYWORDS OF THE SUIT

GYRENE	
TTIOVNOAMI	
PISAONS	
SOPPEUR	
IRILSTAIUYTP	
IEADS	
HTSRTGEN	
IMRTTNIEONDAE	
EIRF	
NNRSTOIIAIP	

WORD SCRAMBLE

Look carefully at the jumbled words and try unscrambling as many of the anagrams as you can into real words. The jumbled words have a theme of the positive expression for the Suit of Wands.

TAROT TILES
REBUILD THE SENTENCE OR PHRASE

Th_ s__t _f W_nds r_pr_s_nts th_ _n_rg_ _f
m_v_m_nt, cr__t_v_t_, _d__s, _nn_v_t__n,
_ntr_pr_n__r__l sp_r_t, _nd _nv_nt__n.

HINT: SUIT OF PASSION

_____

_____

_____

_____

_____

_____

_____

_____

MISSING VOWELS

Can you rebuild the phrase? Fill in the missing vowels to complete
the phrase.

SUITS

P		S	
C			P
	C	P	
	P		W

SUPER EASY SUDOKU

This simplified version of Sudoku uses letters instead of numbers. The letters represent the four suits of the Minor Arcana. The objective is to fill the grid with digits so that each column, each row, and each of the four sub-grids contain all of the letters:

P=PENTACLES S=SWORDS W=WANDS C=CUPS

FIND THE DIFFERENCE

CAN YOU FIND THE DIFFERENCES
BETWEEN THESE TWO REVERSED IMAGES?

THERE ARE 18 DIFFERENCES

SUIT OF WANDS

ACE OF WANDS

D									T								
F	Q	T	I	P		U	H	F	O	A	C	T	I	U	C	T	A H

	O				W		B							
M	A	Q	U	H	P	Z	J	P	K	T	H	H	T	H K

			E		N			F			R			
U	Q	P	J	P	T	H	K	A	M	M	P	Q	P	F

		H							M			.
C	A	E	P	B	D	G	A	X	O	A	I	P .

ACE of WANDS.

TWO OF WANDS

			F										
P	G	B	W	Z	P	Z	M	B		G	E	I	F O

P											S	.		M					
H	E	O	O	T	Q	T	I	T	P	T	B O	.	D	S	N	B		P G B

		H						T						O		
Y	G	E	T	Y	B		P	E		D	S	N	B	C	E	Z M

		V		.
D	E	X	B	.

CRYPTOGRAM

Decode this short piece of encrypted text related to each card. Cryptograms can often be solved by frequency analysis, and by recognizing letter patterns in words, such as one letter words, which, in English, can only be "i" or "a". Hints and punctuation are given for each card.

SUIT OF WANDS

THREE OF WANDS

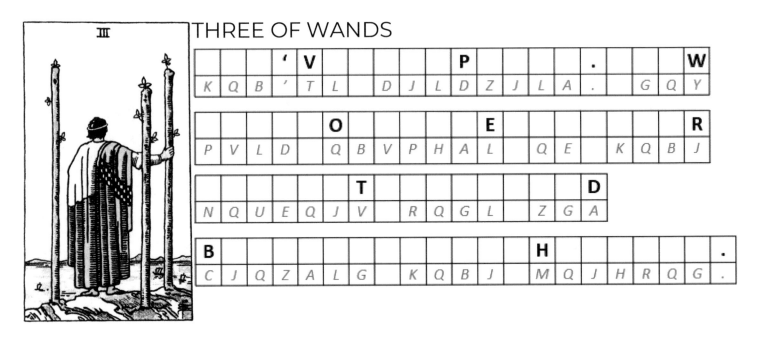

			'	**V**							**P**					.				**W**
K	Q	B	'	T	L		D	J	L	D	Z	J	L	A	.		G	Q	Y

				O							**E**						**R**
P	V	L	D		Q	B	V	P	H	A	L		Q	E		K	Q	B	J

					T								**D**		
N	Q	U	E	Q	J	V		R	Q	G	L		Z	G	A

B												**H**						.
C	J	Q	Z	A	L	G		K	Q	B	J		M	Q	J	H	R	Q	G	.

FOUR OF WANDS

M											**A**								
S	M	T	V	L	C	U	Q	V	L		Z	D	X	V		K	V	V	Q

	E		.		**C**										
S	V	C	.		W	V	T	V	K	Y	D	C	V		D	Q	N

		J							**O**					
V	Q	O	U	A		C	Z	V		S	U	S	V	Q	C

B									**I**				**N**	.
K	V	G	U	Y	V		S	U	X	M	Q	J		U	Q	.

CRYPTOGRAM

Decode this short piece of encrypted text related to each card. Cryptograms can often be solved by frequency analysis, and by recognizing letter patterns in words, such as one letter words, which, in English, can only be "i" or "a". Hints and punctuation are given for each card.

SUIT OF WANDS

FIVE OF WANDS

W						E				A		U			
O	G	R	E		R	S	F		O	F		R	S	M	V	Q	A	M

	B					?				S						G			
R	D	Y	V	E	?		Q	L		L	Y	P	F	E	G	Q	A	M		Q	A

	O										C						I			
Z	Y	V	S		O	R	Z		Y	S		U	Y	P	N	F	E	Q	A	M

	T					?	
O	Q	E	G		Z	Y	V	?

SIX OF WANDS

H					K					D	
W	U	F	O		I	A	F	Q		W	U	K		H	U	S	O

	F		.			J						
A	M	M	.		V	E	B	A	C		R	W	V

	E			-							V						
I	V	X	X	-	O	V	K	V	F	J	V	O		J	S	P	R	A	F	C

A									T				.		R			L
U	E	O		F	V	P	A	T	E	S	R	S	A	E	.		F	V	J	V	X

				I		.
S	E		S	R	.

CRYPTOGRAM

Decode this short piece of encrypted text related to each card. Cryptograms can often be solved by frequency analysis, and by recognizing letter patterns in words, such as one letter words, which, in English, can only be "i" or "a". Hints and punctuation are given for each card.

SUIT OF WANDS

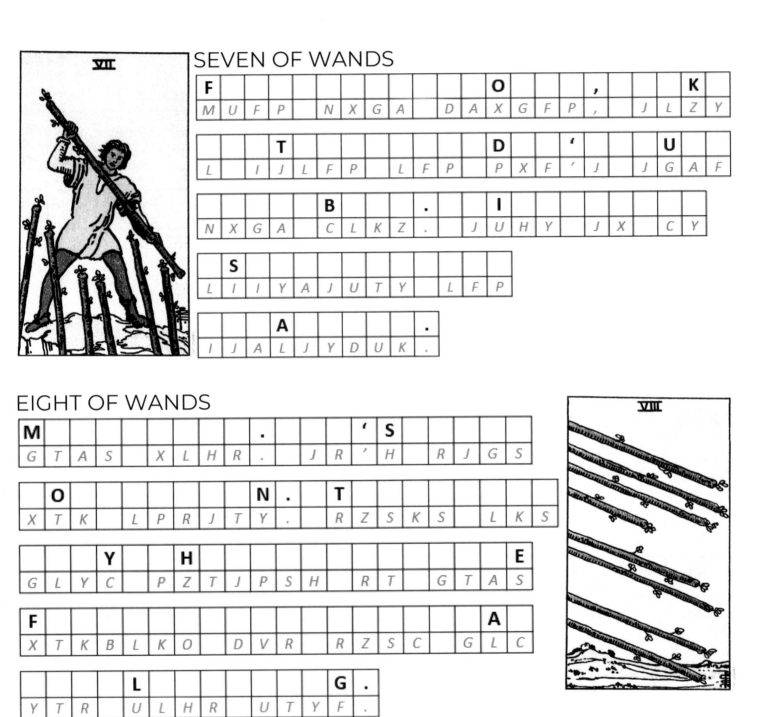

SEVEN OF WANDS

F											O					,				K	
M	U	F	P		N	X	G	A		D	A	X	G	F	P	,		J	L	Z	Y

		T									D			'				U			
L		I	J	L	F	P		L	F	P	P	X	F	'	J		J	G	A	F	

			B					.			I									
N	X	G	A		C	L	K	Z	.		J	U	H	Y		J	X		C	Y

	S										
L	I	I	Y	A	J	U	T	Y		L	F	P

		A						.	
I	J	A	L	J	Y	D	U	K	.

EIGHT OF WANDS

M								.			'	S					
G	T	A	S		X	L	H	R	.		J	R	'	H		R	J	G	S

	O						N	.		T							
X	T	K		L	P	R	J	T	Y	.		R	Z	S	K	S		L	K	S

		Y		H										E
G	L	Y	C		P	Z	T	J	P	S	H		R	T		G	T	A	S

F													A	
X	T	K	B	L	K	O		D	V	R		R	Z	S	C		G	L	C

			L						G	.
Y	T	R		U	L	H	R		U	T	Y	F	.

CRYPTOGRAM

Decode this short piece of encrypted text related to each card. Cryptograms can often be solved by frequency analysis, and by recognizing letter patterns in words, such as one letter words, which, in English, can only be "i" or "a". Hints and punctuation are given for each card.

SUIT OF WANDS

NINE OF WANDS

I		'				E							T		
K	Y	'	W		Y	V	M		I	H	W	Y		W	Y	H	R	X

				Y			'									L			
H	R	X		P	E	F	'	C	M		T	E	L	M		H		I	E	R	J

W			.					D				
B	H	P	.		Y	V	M		M	R	X		K	W

A								G			.
H	I	L	E	W	Y		K	R		W	K	J	V	Y	.

TEN OF WANDS

T	'						Y					.			O
R	A	'	V		K		G	D	K	J	C		W	X	K	P	.		P	X

			E				P			
C	X	H		I	D	D	P		G	D	W	U		T	R	A	G

V								U	'	
D	J	D	Q	C	A	G	R	I	E		C	X	H	'	Q	D

A				?				J			
S	K	Q	Q	C	R	I	E	?		A	G	D		B	X	H	Q	I	D	C

S		L					.
R	V		K	W	F	X	V	A		X	J	D	Q	.

CRYPTOGRAM

Decode this short piece of encrypted text related to each card. Cryptograms can often be solved by frequency analysis, and by recognizing letter patterns in words, such as one letter words, which, in English, can only be "i" or "a". Hints and punctuation are given for each card.

SUIT OF WANDS

PAGE OF WANDS

				E															
E	J	P		X	C	R		Q	J	I		O	V	J	C	I		J	Q

C										**,**
B	P	C	Y	J	O	Y	I	E		,

			I							**,**				**W**			
Y	Q	O	T	Y	C	X	I	Y	J	Q	,		J	C		K	X	E	O

		X											**S**					**.**
I	J		R	F	T	C	R	O	O		E	J	P	C	O	R	H	A	.

A					**R**				**Y**	**.**
W	X	T		X		O	I	C	X	I	R	S	E	.

PAGE of WANDS.

KNIGHT OF WANDS

KNIGHT of WANDS.

W										**A**								
O	Q	J	Q		P	T	F		O	R	V	G	V	D	U		Y	T	J

			G											**T**	
G	I	Q		U	J	Q	Q	D		C	V	U	I		G	T

	R									**E**					
A	J	V	D	U		P	T	F	J		D	Q	O		V	W	Q	R

	F							**?**	**S**					**N**		**!**
G	T		Y	J	F	V	G	V	T	D	?	K	G	R	J	G		D	T	O	!

CRYPTOGRAM

Decode this short piece of encrypted text related to each card. Cryptograms can often be solved by frequency analysis, and by recognizing letter patterns in words, such as one letter words, which, in English, can only be "i" or "a". Hints and punctuation are given for each card.

SUIT OF WANDS

QUEEN of WANDS.

QUEEN OF WANDS

Y																		W		.
T	Y	R	Q		V	Y	U	S	B	L	P	U	V	P		F	Z	Y	D	F

				E								R								,
T	Y	R		P	G	M	Y	L	T		V	Q	P	J	K	B	X	B	K	T

	M								
P	G	Y	K	B	Y	U	J	H	

	N									,		A			
B	U	K	P	H	H	B	O	P	U	V	P	,		J	U	L

H					-			T						C					.
Z	P	J	Q	K	-	V	P	U	K	P	Q	P	L		J	V	K	B	Y	U	F

KING OF WANDS

	N								O									
L		V	L	Y	Z	K	L	T		N	J	K	V		T	F	L	H	F	K

			C						
L	V	H		S	K	F	L	Y	E	X	F

V								,					R		
X	E	B	E	J	V	L	K	A	,		A	J	Z		L	K	F

	E							K				A			
K	F	L	H	A		Y	J		Y	L	D	F		S	C	L	K	P	F

			D						T				.
L	V	H		H	E	K	F	S	Y		J	Y	C	F	K	B	.

KING of WANDS

CRYPTOGRAM

Decode this short piece of encrypted text related to each card. Cryptograms can often be solved by frequency analysis, and by recognizing letter patterns in words, such as one letter words, which, in English, can only be "i" or "a". Hints and punctuation are given for each card.

TAROT TILES

REBUILD THE SENTENCE OR PHRASE

P_g_s c_nc__v_ _d__s, Kn_ghts _ct _p_n _d__s,
Q___ns n_rt_r_ _d__s _nd n_w K_ngs d_v_l_p
th_s_ _d__s t_ _n _st_bl_sh_d _nd st_bl_ st_t_.

HINT: COURT CARDS

_____

_____

_____

_____

_____

_____

_____

_____

_____

MISSING VOWELS

Can you rebuild the phrase? Fill in the missing vowels to complete the phrase.

FINISH THE PICTURE

KNIGHT of CUPS.

THE PAGE

CHARACTERISTICS OF THE COURT CARDS

Court cards in the Minor Arcana can represent the energy of a person, an event, or a situation that's taken on a personality or a life of its own, or even the maturity level of someone's mindset. They are generally gender-neutral regardless of the representation on the card. Emphasis is placed more on the information they carry.

Since they have mastered the lessons of the Ace through Ten cards before them and carry the wisdom of those lessons learned, each card represents the next level of energy.

They are the final stages of a journey with the Page as the beginning and the King as the end of the journey.

A Page is a novice, ready to step into the action and gain the experience of the Knight that follows. The energy of a Page is similar to that of a young energetic person, curious and ready to learn and step into their own.

The keywords below are the characteristics of the Page card.

LOCATE THE FOLLOWING WORDS IN THE WORD ZIG ZAG ON THE NEXT PAGE:

- CHILDLIKE
- ENERGETIC
- JOY
- LEARNING
- OPPORTUNITY
- PRACTICING
- REBIRTH
- TRANSFORMATION
- WANDER
- YOUNG

THE PAGE

B	E	R	N	R	N	A	R	T	Y	O	J
I	M	C	H	I	S	F	O	M	A	Y	O
R	V	P	P	L	L	Z	R	L	E	A	U
T	H	Z	P	D	L	Y	M	A	O	R	N
A	E	J	R	X	I	K	E	T	I	N	G
G	N	B	A	C	C	N	O	I	N	D	U
H	E	R	G	T	I	O	P	P	G	I	V
A	W	E	E	T	C	K	S	O	N	O	Y
N	P	M	F	I	I	T	L	R	W	E	T
D	E	R	R	C	N	G	R	T	U	N	I

WORD ZIGZAG

A different kind of word search. These words aren't in a straight line. The letters zig zag up and down. Look for words with their letters connected on the top, bottom, left, and right (but not diagonally) to find the words listed on the previous page.

THE KNIGHT

CHARACTERISTICS OF THE COURT CARDS

Court cards in the Minor Arcana can represent the energy of a person, an event, or a situation that's taken on a personality or a life of its own, or even the maturity level of someone's mindset. They are generally gender-neutral regardless of the representation on the card. Emphasis is placed more on the information they carry.

Since they have mastered the lessons of the Ace through Ten cards before them and carry the wisdom of those lessons learned, each card represents the next level of energy.

They are the final stages of a journey with the Page as the beginning and the King as the end of the journey. Use your intuition to decide!

The Knight represents action and speed and laser like focus, eager to master this level so they can move on to the next. A Knights energy is similar to that of a young adult.

The keywords below are the characteristics of the Knight card.

LOCATE THE FOLLOWING WORDS IN THE WORD ZIG ZAG ON THE NEXT PAGE:

- ACTION
- CHANGE
- EXPERIENCE
- EXTREMISTS
- JOURNEY
- MOVEMENT
- OPPORTUNITY
- REVELATION
- UNDERWAY
- YOUNG ADULT

THE KNIGHT

O	P	P	O	E	X	Y	O	U	N	F	E
R	T	A	T	I	T	C	H	T	G	P	X
T	U	C	Y	R	R	E	A	L	A	E	A
D	N	T	I	O	E	M	N	U	D	R	G
Y	I	T	X	N	Z	I	G	E	E	I	H
B	V	Y	T	X	R	S	E	C	N	P	M
I	T	A	L	E	S	T	C	U	E	V	O
O	J	O	U	V	E	R	D	N	M	O	K
N	P	L	R	J	Y	A	E	U	E	S	M
M	N	L	N	E	Y	W	R	T	N	W	I

WORD ZIGZAG

A different kind of word search. These words aren't in a straight line. The letters zig zag up and down. Look for words with their letters connected on the top, bottom, left, and right (but not diagonally) to find the words listed on the previous page.

THE PAGE

CHARACTERISTICS OF THE COURT CARDS

The Page refers to our childlike ability to see the magic in the world and our eagerness to learn about new areas. They represent youth, vitality, and learning.

PAGE of WANDS.

PAGE of SWORDS.

- the practical world, entrepreneurship, professional training, stability

- intellectual pursuits, becoming a student, information, communication

- creativity, rebuilding, new skills, learn by doing

- a new life, intuition, spirituality, guidance, relationships

PAGE of CUPS.

PAGE of PENTACLES.

MATCHING

Draw a line to match the Page with their interest according to the characteristic of the suit.

THE KNIGHT
CHARACTERISTICS OF THE COURT CARDS

The Knight refers to speed with which events occur, head-strong, risk-taking and full of action. They bring an energy of enthusiasm and the desire to get things done.

- quest for physical objects, practical, slow, deliberate

- quest for passion, desire, anxious to leap in to get started, forward energy

- quest for love, romantic, sweep you off your feet, emo poet

- quest for philosophical, new ideas, communication, rational thought

MATCHING

Draw a line to match the Knight with their interest according to the characteristic of the suit.

THE QUEEN
CHARACTERISTICS OF THE COURT CARDS

Court cards in the Minor Arcana can represent the energy of a person, an event, or a situation that's taken on a personality or a life of its own, or even the maturity level of someone's mindset. They are generally gender-neutral regardless of the representation on the card. Emphasis is placed more on the information they carry.

Since they have mastered the lessons of the Ace through Ten cards before them and carry the wisdom of those lessons learned, each card represents the next level of energy.

They are the final stages of a journey with the Page as the beginning and the King as the end of the journey. Use your intuition to decide!

The Queen is very receiving, mature and self-aware. She is gentle and able to influence others without their knowing. Her energy is that of a mature woman with enough experience behind her but plenty of time left to learn more and level up to a King.

The keywords below are the characteristics of the Queen card.

LOCATE THE FOLLOWING WORDS IN THE WORD ZIG ZAG ON THE NEXT PAGE:

- CARING
- FEMININE
- GENTLE INFLUENCE
- MATURE
- NOURISHMENT

- NURTURING
- PERSUASIVE
- POWERFUL
- SUSTENANCE
- UNDERSTANDING

THE QUEEN

P	K	S	I	R	U	N	E	G	S	U	S
E	C	H	G	J	O	T	P	L	E	F	T
R	A	M	E	S	N	L	O	U	M	N	E
S	R	I	N	S	D	E	W	F	I	A	N
U	A	N	T	F	N	I	E	R	N	G	C
M	S	G	G	L	E	E	E	N	I	N	E
O	I	V	E	U	N	U	R	U	B	I	C
M	A	T	S	E	N	A	T	N	G	D	N
M	E	U	H	S	C	R	U	D	E	F	A
Z	C	R	E	H	E	I	N	G	R	S	T

WORD ZIGZAG

A different kind of word search. These words aren't in a straight line. The letters zig zag up and down. Look for words with their letters connected on the top, bottom, left, and right (but not diagonally) to find the words listed on the previous page.

THE KING
CHARACTERISTICS OF THE COURT CARDS

Court cards in the Minor Arcana can represent the energy of a person, an event, or a situation that has taken on a personality or a life of its own, or even the maturity level of someone's mindset. They are generally gender-neutral regardless of the representation on the card. Emphasis is placed more on the information they carry.

Since they have mastered the lessons of the Ace through Ten cards before them and carry the wisdom of those lessons learned, each card represents the next level of energy.

They are the final stages of a journey with the Page as the beginning and the King as the end of the journey. Use your intuition to decide!

This King carries the energy of an mature male, successful at the height of their life, exuding power and leadership from their knowledge. They have experience as a provider with a stable energy in control in all areas.

The keywords below are the characteristics of the King card.

LOCATE THE FOLLOWING WORDS IN THE WORD ZIG ZAG ON THE NEXT PAGE:

- CONTROL
- DIRECT
- EXPERIENCE
- MASCULINE
- MATURE
- PROVIDER
- RESPONSIBLE
- SOLID
- STABLE
- UNDERSTANDING

THE KING

O	G	H	A	S	C	U	J	P	G	J	R
C	O	N	M	N	O	L	U	R	I	D	E
U	L	T	N	S	P	I	N	O	V	F	K
N	O	R	A	I	S	N	D	S	T	A	N
D	L	E	L	B	E	E	E	R	B	O	D
L	I	D	M	D	R	C	G	H	U	T	I
O	M	T	T	A	T	S	Z	E	R	A	N
S	H	E	C	B	O	E	E	I	R	M	G
R	I	R	E	L	E	C	N	G	E	S	T
N	D	P	M	E	F	L	S	T	P	X	E

WORD ZIGZAG

A different kind of word search. These words aren't in a straight line. The letters zig zag up and down. Look for words with their letters connected on the top, bottom, left, and right (but not diagonally) to find the words listed on the previous page.

THE QUEEN

CHARACTERISTICS OF THE COURT CARDS

The Queen represents openness and expressiveness. They are incredibly in tune with themselves and ask us to see how we are using our abilities, and if we are using our power creatively rather than authoritatively.

- nurturing of the environment, aids others, wants to better the world, connected

- nurturing intellect, understanding of the world, formidable, trusted advisor

- nurturing passion, creative, dependable, independent, grounded, confident

- nurturing love, caring, natural healer, holds space for others

MATCHING

Draw a line to match the Queen with their interest according to the characteristic of the suit.

THE KING

CHARACTERISTICS OF THE COURT CARDS

The King is fully in control, having mastered their suit with hard work and dedication. They project their expertise and power outward. They have earned respect and their place in this leadership position.

- philosopher, enjoys concepts, principles, knowledge, planning,

- forerunners, they value change, innovation, creativity, new ideas

- poets, understanding, interpersonal dynamics, feeling, perceptive, intuitive

- strong command of resources and money, shares wealth with others

MATCHING

Draw a line to match the King with their interest according to the characteristic of the suit.

REVERSALS

IT'S IN THE CARDS

The keywords and descriptions used in this book have been mostly for the card energy and characteristics of a card in the upright position. Often, cards appear in an upside-down or a reversed position during a reading.

Tarot readers have different opinions on the meanings of a reversed card, however, most agree that the meaning varies based on your intuition. Some tarot readers choose not to read reversals at all, while others feel it adds depth and insight to a reading.

Here are some thoughts on how some readers see reversals.

Pause or wait: Someone may not be at the exact stage to realize the message of the upright card. There may be a waiting period or another event that needs to happen first. *Example: The Knight of Pentacles reversed could mean a new job is forthcoming but taking longer than expected.*

A block: There could be an energetic block either consciously or subconsciously relating to the message of the upright card. Ask if anything is getting in the way of the upright energy of the card. *Example: The Ace of Cups reversed could mean a new relationship is possible but they must put energy into loving themself first.*

REVERSALS

IT'S IN THE CARDS

Internal vs external: Upright energy is expressed outwardly into the world externally. Someone may be internalizing privately or secretly. *Example: The Empress reversed could mean that they need to take care of themself rather than taking care of others.*

Upside-down imagery: Look at the card's images for an intuitive hit. *Example: The Page of Pentacles reversed could appear as if the coins are slipping out of the hands rather than being caught.*

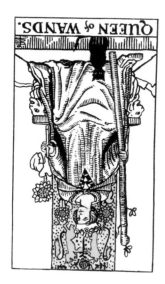

Imbalance: There may exist too little or too much energy of the upright card. *Example: A Queen of Wands reversed could mean over-confidence and domineering, or conversely shyness in public situations.*

SUIT OF WANDS

NEGATIVE EXPRESSIONS & REVERSALS

Every suit of the Minor Arcana carries positive and negative expressions. Positive expressions (upright cards) could contribute to the success of an event, while negative expressions (reversed cards) could take away from it.

For example, for Wands, a positive expression might be passion and enthusiasm while a negative expression might be impatience and being hot-tempered.

The keywords below are negative expressions of the Suit of Wands.

LOCATE THE FOLLOWING WORDS IN THE WORD ZIG ZAG ON THE NEXT PAGE:

- AGGRESSIVE
- BRASH
- COCKY
- HASTY
- HEADSTRONG
- IMPATIENT
- OVERCONFIDENT
- RECKLESS
- THOUGHTLESS
- UNPREPARED

SUIT OF WANDS

NEGATIVE EXPRESSIONS & REVERSALS

C	O	S	E	R	G	G	A	T	C	O	E
H	V	S	E	B	R	A	E	H	K	C	D
R	E	I	V	E	U	S	H	O	Y	N	U
C	O	N	F	A	B	K	S	S	M	P	R
T	A	B	I	D	E	U	O	I	N	G	E
H	H	Z	H	A	N	T	Y	M	P	H	P
O	E	D	T	S	T	S	I	T	A	R	A
U	A	D	S	T	Y	S	E	G	H	E	R
G	N	S	S	R	G	T	N	T	T	C	E
H	T	L	E	O	N	S	S	E	L	K	D

WORD ZIGZAG

A different kind of word search. These words aren't in a straight line. The letters zig zag up and down. Look for words with their letters connected on the top, bottom, left, and right (but not diagonally) to find the words listed on the previous page.

SUIT OF CUPS

NEGATIVE EXPRESSIONS & REVERSALS

Every suit of the Minor Arcana carries positive and negative expressions. Positive expressions (upright cards) could contribute to the success of an event, while negative expressions (reversed cards could take away from it.

For example, a positive expression for the suit of Cups would be loving and emotionally stable, while a negative expression may be dispassionate or unrealistic expectations.

The keywords below are negative expressions of the Suit of Cups.

LOCATE THE FOLLOWING WORDS IN THE WORD ZIG ZAG ON THE NEXT PAGE:

- DELICATE
- FRAGILE
- HUFFY
- HYSTERICAL
- INTROVERTED
- LAZY
- MOODY
- NARCISSISTIC
- PASSIVE
- TOUCHY

SUIT OF CUPS

NEGATIVE EXPRESSIONS & REVERSALS

P	L	D	Z	F	H	C	A	I	O	O	D
A	A	E	L	R	Y	U	F	N	I	N	T
S	T	E	I	A	Y	O	F	T	Y	H	R
S	E	Z	C	G	I	T	T	R	S	V	O
I	V	T	A	N	L	S	R	E	T	E	A
A	D	E	I	A	E	S	I	M	T	R	R
H	U	E	V	R	G	H	C	A	E	Y	C
F	F	C	S	C	I	C	I	L	D	Z	A
Y	F	Y	S	M	S	N	T	G	O	R	L
L	I	D	O	O	S	I	S	I	C	A	L

WORD ZIGZAG

A different kind of word search. These words aren't in a straight line. The letters zig zag up and down. Look for words with their letters connected on the top, bottom, left, and right (but not diagonally) to find the words listed on the previous page.

SUIT OF PENTACLES

NEGATIVE EXPRESSIONS & REVERSALS

Every suit of the Minor Arcana carries positive and negative expressions. Positive expressions (upright cards) could contribute to the success of an event, while negative expressions (reversed cards) could take away from it.

For example, a positive expression for the suit of Pentacles might be abundance and career, while a negative expression might be lack of trust or a business failure.

The keywords below are negative expressions of the Suit of Pentacles.

LOCATE THE FOLLOWING WORDS IN THE WORD ZIG ZAG ON THE NEXT PAGE:

- COMPULSIVE
- CONVENTIONAL
- INFLEXIBLE
- MATERIALISTIC
- OBSESSIVE
- PERFECTIONIST
- RIGID
- STUBBORN
- TIMID
- UNADVENTUROUS

SUIT OF PENTACLES
NEGATIVE EXPRESSIONS & REVERSALS

D	I	M	I	T	N	T	A	M	N	F	I
C	O	S	I	R	O	E	B	B	I	L	D
U	M	L	V	U	U	R	I	A	F	E	S
N	P	U	E	T	S	L	A	L	I	X	T
A	D	V	E	N	I	T	S	I	B	S	U
C	O	N	V	E	C	A	D	E	L	B	B
F	R	E	P	N	C	E	S	S	U	O	T
E	S	T	Z	T	L	S	I	I	B	R	N
C	I	N	F	I	A	B	S	V	E	O	R
T	I	O	L	O	N	O	S	D	I	G	I

WORD ZIGZAG

A different kind of word search. These words aren't in a straight line. The letters zig zag up and down. Look for words with their letters connected on the top, bottom, left, and right (but not diagonally) to find the words listed on the previous page.

SUIT OF SWORDS
NEGATIVE EXPRESSIONS & REVERSALS

Every suit of the Minor Arcana carries positive and negative expressions. Positive expressions (upright cards) could contribute to the success of an event, while negative expressions (reversed cards) could take away from it.

For example, for Swords, a positive expression might be ambition and courage, while a negative expression may be anger, guilt or lack of compassion.

The keywords below are negative expressions of the Suit of Swords.

LOCATE THE FOLLOWING WORDS IN THE WORD ZIG ZAG ON THE NEXT PAGE:

- ALOOF
- ARROGANT
- BLUNT
- COLD
- CUTTING
- DOGMATIC
- INSENSITIVE
- JUDGMENTAL
- OVERBEARING
- UNFEELING

SUIT OF SWORDS

NEGATIVE EXPRESSIONS & REVERSALS

A	O	O	M	P	A	L	L	N	E	I	N
C	Z	A	R	R	D	O	T	U	C	I	S
D	U	J	C	O	F	O	T	E	S	D	E
G	M	O	A	G	R	Z	I	E	T	O	N
B	E	N	N	Y	R	G	N	B	M	G	S
C	O	T	T	T	U	D	G	T	A	T	I
D	L	A	M	T	G	N	M	I	S	I	A
A	R	L	B	L	U	I	L	C	E	V	L
U	N	G	N	I	N	R	A	E	N	E	O
N	F	E	E	L	T	N	G	B	R	E	V

WORD ZIGZAG

A different kind of word search. These words aren't in a straight line. The letters zig zag up and down. Look for words with their letters connected on the top, bottom, left, and right (but not diagonally) to find the words listed on the previous page.

ANSWERS

FILL IN THE BLANK ANSWERS

TAROT CARDS AS A DIVINATION TOOL

Tarot cards have been used as a divination tool since the early sixteenth century starting in the country of **Italy**. They were developed as a tool to demonstrate the various **cycles** of life as in the Major Arcana, and then also as a way to explain the various stages of each of the four major **emotions** people encounter in life such as thoughts and ideas (Swords), emotions (Cups), Passion and purpose (Wands) and material possessions (Pentacles).

The tarot card deck is meant to walk an individual through the **beginning** of a cycle to the completion of a cycle, only to start again when the next occasion arises. There are many **symbols** and meanings involved with each card that can leave an inexperienced reader confused. It takes time and **patience** to understand the entire deck but it is possible to master with enough study and learning to use your intuition. There are many ways to learn to read. You must find the way that works for you.

The tarot deck can be used to receive messages from your **higher self** as well as from your guides. They use the deck to convey messages to the reader. It is only **one** of the ways for guides to relay messages, but it is an easy way for guides if the reader understands how to interpret the message. They may answer a certain question from the reader, or they may simply relay a needed message. **Multiple** card spreads are used to relay extended messages over many cards.

The message is meant for that particular **moment** in time, based on the circumstances at that same moment in time. Because every human has **free will**, the message can change at any time - because something has changed with the person the message is meant for. The message is strictly meant for that moment.

Contrary to movies or television, tarot cards are not working with the dark arts but are instead working with **Spirit**. Tarot cards cannot predict the **future** and they cannot give any insight into the past reasoning for certain actions. They are a fun way to connect to Spirit and are sure to come in a **theme** to interest you! The message is strictly meant for that moment.

NUMEROLOGY ANSWERS

1. new beginnings, individual, independence
2. duality, partnership, choice
3. collaboration, community, creativity
4. foundation, structure, stability
5. change, loss, instability
6. harmony, hope, balance
7. intuition, magic, inspired action
8. power, infinity, success
9. growth, near completion, alone
10. wholeness, end of cycle, completion

WORD SEARCH ANSWERS

THE FOOL

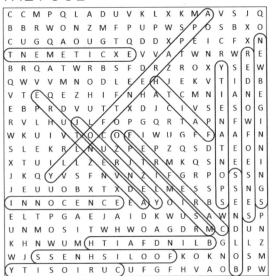

THE MAGICIAN

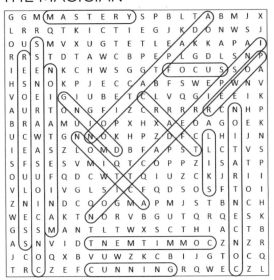

THE HIGH PRIESTESS

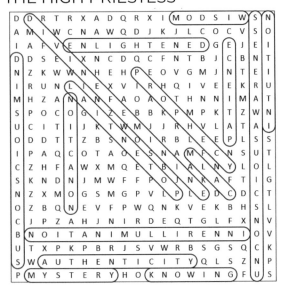

THE EMPRESS

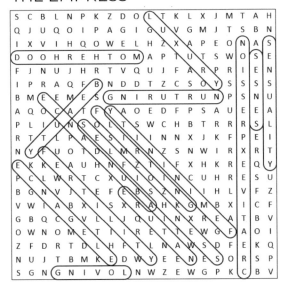

THE EMPEROR

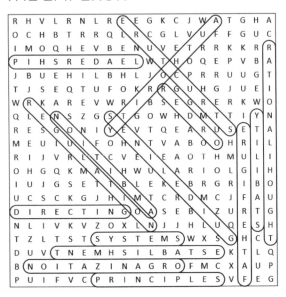

THE HIEROPHANT

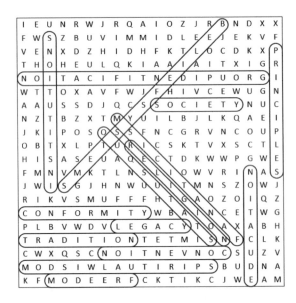

WORD SEARCH ANSWERS

THE LOVERS

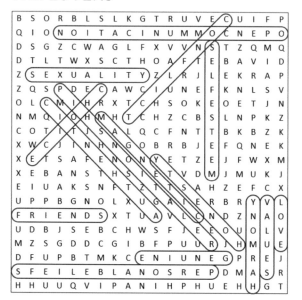

THE CHARIOT

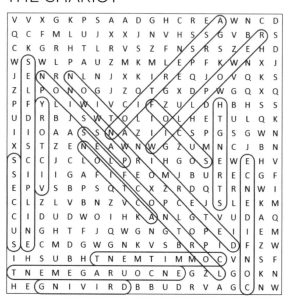

STRENGTH

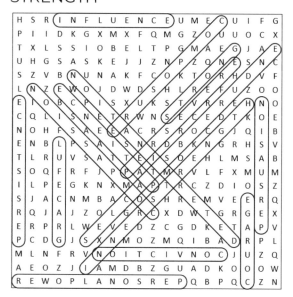

THE HERMIT

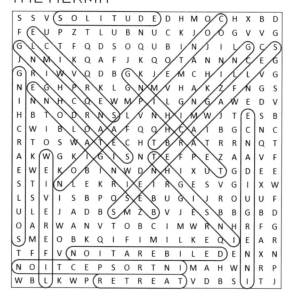

WHEEL OF FORTUNE

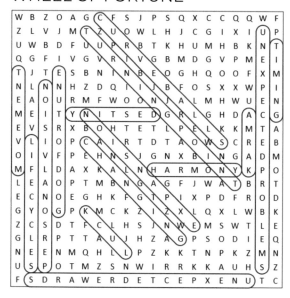

JUSTICE

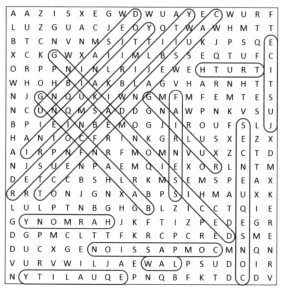

WORD SEARCH ANSWERS

HANGED MAN

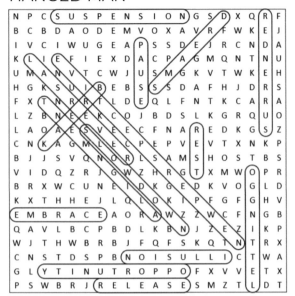

DEATH

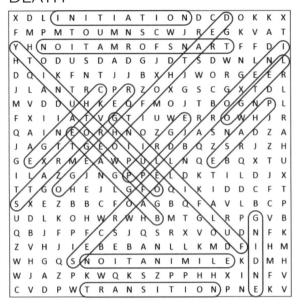

TEMPERANCE

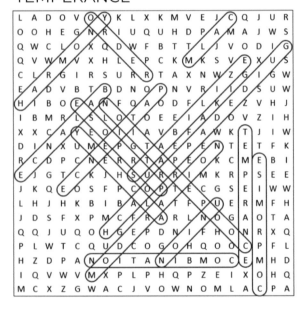

THE DEVIL

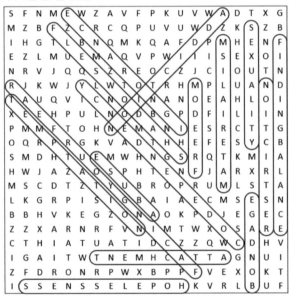

THE TOWER

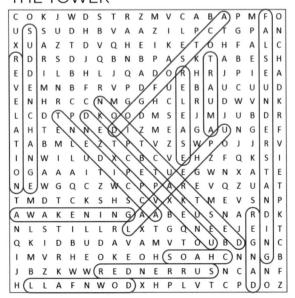

THE STAR

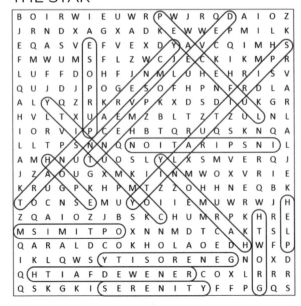

WORD SEARCH ANSWERS

THE MOON

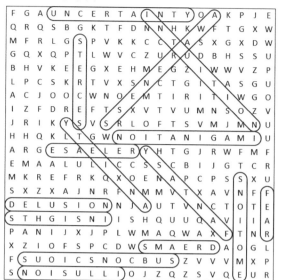

THE SUN

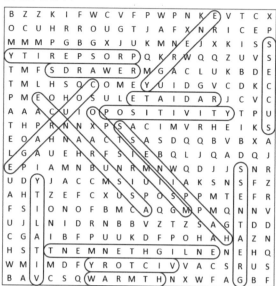

JUDGEMENT

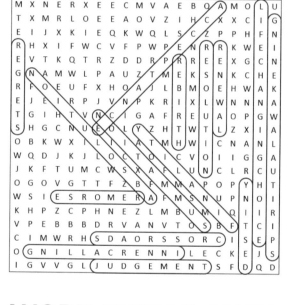

THE WORLD

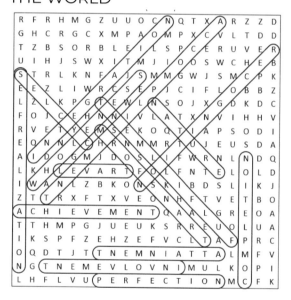

WORD ZIGZAG ANSWERS

WANDS

CUPS

WORD ZIGZAG ANSWERS

PENTACLES

SWORDS

PAGE

KNIGHT

QUEEN

KING

WORD SCRAMBLE ANSWERS

CUPS

IFELNSGE	FEELINGS
MISTOONE	EMOTIONS
NIAOAIMNTIG	IMAGINATION
LSORIPASNETIH	RELATIONSHIPS
LVEO	LOVE
SNCETNNIOOC	CONNECTIONS
WARET	WATER
INTTIIONU	INTUITION
NEIMFNEI	FEMININE
NOMMSIATIRC	ROMANTICISM

PENTACLES

NAFCNESI	FINANCES
REEACR	CAREER
SOPSISSESON	POSSESSIONS
GINTLEAB	TANGIBLE
EATLWH	WEALTH
AELHHT	HEALTH
IEIVYCRATT	CREATIVITY
ERTHA	EARTH
FSIEANTMIANOT	MANIFESTATOIN
PROSTIPYRE	PROSPERITY

SWORDS

UTGOHHTS	THOUGHTS
ORSWD	WORDS
CTNAOSI	ACTIONS
ESDIA	IDEAS
SDOEIINCS	DECISIONS
WEROP	POWER
AENTML	MENTAL
LIEFBE	BELIEF
ATIETDUT	ATTITUDE
OITIBANM	AMBITION

WANDS

GYRENE	ENERGY
TTIOVNOAMI	MOTIVATION
PISAONS	PASSION
SOPPEUR	PURPOSE
IRILSTAIUYTP	SPIRITUALITY
IEADS	IDEAS
HTSRTGEN	STRENGTH
IMRTTNIEONDAE	DETERMINATION
EIRF	FIRE
NNRSTOIIAIP	INSPIRATION

COURT CARDS MATCHING ANSWERS

- Page of Pentacles: the practical world, entrepreneurship, professional training, stability

- Page of Swords: intellectual pursuits, becoming a student, information, communication

- Page of Wands: creativity, rebuilding, new skills, learn by doing

- Page of Cups: a new life, intuition, spirituality, guidance, relationships

- Knight of Pentacles: quest for physical objects, practical, slow, deliberate

- Knight of Wands: quest for passion, desire, anxious to leap in to get started, forward energy

- Knight of Cups: quest for love, romantic, sweep you off your feet, emo poet

- Knight of Swords: quest for philosophical, new ideas, communication, rational thought

- Queen of Pentacles: nurturing of the environment, aids others, wants to better the world, connected

- Queen of Swords: nurturing intellect, understanding of the world, formidable, trusted advisor

- Queen of Wands: nurturing passion, creative, dependable, independent, grounded, confident

- Queen of Cups: nurturing love, caring, natural healer, holds space for others
- King of Swords: philosopher, enjoys concepts, principles, knowledge, planning,

- King of Wands: forerunners, they value change, innovation, creativity, new ideas

- King of Cups: poets, understanding, interpersonal dynamics, feeling, perceptive, intuitive

- King of Pentacles: strong command of resources and money, shares wealth with others

WORD TILES ANSWERS

READING

Each Tarot reading is unique to you at that moment and time because the cards work with your energy which is channeled into the cards and you are drawn to the cards that are most relevant to you.

COMPLIMENTARY FRIENDS

Numerology allows you to understand the power lurking in numbers and indicates that some things in life may be interconnected. Tarot unlocks life with symbols, allows you to interpret yourself, your life, and your future, and improve your intuition.

MAJOR ARCANA

The Major Arcana Tarot cards represent the life lessons, karmic influences and the big archetypal themes that are influencing your life and your soul's journey to enlightenment.

WORD TILES ANSWERS

RELATIONSHIPS
Numerology is the belief in a divine or mystical relationship between a number and one or more coinciding events.

DIFFERENCES
Tarot cards depend on symbolism and Numerology depends on numbers which may sound simple but are actually complex systems of divination.

COURT CARDS
Pages conceive ideas, Knights act upon ideas, Queens nurture ideas and now Kings develop those ideas to an established and stable state.

SUIT OF EMOTION
The suit of Cups is connected to our emotions, our relationships, and matters of the soul.

SUIT OF PASSION
The suit of Wands represents the energy of movement, creativity, ideas, innovation, entrepreneurial spirit, and invention.

SUIT OF LOGIC
The Swords suit helps you prepare for life's greatest challenges, and remind you of your own knowledge and strength.

SUIT OF SUCCESS
The Pentacles suit pertains to things in the material and physical world such as wealth and money but also to success and prosperity such as career success, family, body, and health matters.

WORD SUDOKU ANSWERS

EASY

TAROT	AIR	CUPS	EARTH	WANDS	WATER	SWORDS	FIRE	COINS
EARTH	FIRE	WATER	CUPS	COINS	SWORDS	WANDS	AIR	TAROT
COINS	SWORDS	WANDS	FIRE	TAROT	AIR	EARTH	CUPS	WATER
CUPS	WANDS	TAROT	AIR	FIRE	COINS	WATER	SWORDS	EARTH
AIR	WATER	COINS	SWORDS	EARTH	WANDS	CUPS	TAROT	FIRE
SWORDS	EARTH	FIRE	TAROT	WATER	CUPS	AIR	COINS	WANDS
WATER	TAROT	SWORDS	COINS	AIR	EARTH	FIRE	WANDS	CUPS
FIRE	CUPS	EARTH	WANDS	SWORDS	TAROT	COINS	WATER	AIR
WANDS	COINS	AIR	WATER	CUPS	FIRE	TAROT	EARTH	SWORDS

EASY

FIRE	COINS	WANDS	WATER	EARTH	SWORDS	CUPS	AIR	TAROT
SWORDS	TAROT	CUPS	COINS	WANDS	AIR	WATER	FIRE	EARTH
AIR	EARTH	WATER	TAROT	FIRE	CUPS	COINS	SWORDS	WANDS
WANDS	SWORDS	EARTH	AIR	TAROT	COINS	FIRE	WATER	CUPS
WATER	AIR	FIRE	CUPS	SWORDS	EARTH	WANDS	TAROT	COINS
COINS	CUPS	TAROT	FIRE	WATER	WANDS	AIR	EARTH	SWORDS
CUPS	WATER	COINS	EARTH	AIR	TAROT	SWORDS	WANDS	FIRE
TAROT	FIRE	SWORDS	WANDS	CUPS	WATER	EARTH	COINS	AIR
EARTH	WANDS	AIR	SWORDS	COINS	FIRE	TAROT	CUPS	WATER

WORD SUDOKU ANSWERS

INTERMEDIATE

COINS	CUPS	FIRE	WANDS	WATER	SWORDS	EARTH	AIR	TAROT
SWORDS	TAROT	WATER	COINS	EARTH	AIR	CUPS	FIRE	WANDS
EARTH	AIR	WANDS	CUPS	FIRE	TAROT	SWORDS	COINS	WATER
CUPS	FIRE	COINS	SWORDS	WANDS	WATER	TAROT	EARTH	AIR
TAROT	SWORDS	AIR	FIRE	CUPS	EARTH	WATER	WANDS	COINS
WATER	WANDS	EARTH	AIR	TAROT	COINS	FIRE	CUPS	SWORDS
WANDS	COINS	CUPS	WATER	SWORDS	FIRE	AIR	TAROT	EARTH
AIR	EARTH	SWORDS	TAROT	COINS	CUPS	WANDS	WATER	FIRE
FIRE	WATER	TAROT	EARTH	AIR	WANDS	COINS	SWORDS	CUPS

HARD

WATER	EARTH	COINS	AIR	FIRE	SWORDS	CUPS	TAROT	WANDS
FIRE	TAROT	SWORDS	EARTH	CUPS	WANDS	COINS	AIR	WATER
CUPS	WANDS	AIR	COINS	TAROT	WATER	SWORDS	EARTH	FIRE
EARTH	SWORDS	TAROT	FIRE	AIR	CUPS	WANDS	WATER	COINS
WANDS	FIRE	WATER	SWORDS	COINS	EARTH	AIR	CUPS	TAROT
COINS	AIR	CUPS	WATER	WANDS	TAROT	EARTH	FIRE	SWORDS
AIR	CUPS	WANDS	TAROT	SWORDS	FIRE	WATER	COINS	EARTH
SWORDS	WATER	FIRE	CUPS	EARTH	COINS	TAROT	WANDS	AIR
TAROT	COINS	EARTH	WANDS	WATER	AIR	FIRE	SWORDS	CUPS

SUPER EASY SUDOKU ANSWERS

ELEMENTS

F	W	A	E
A	E	W	F
W	F	E	A
E	A	F	W

ELEMENTS

A	E	F	W
W	F	E	A
E	W	A	F
F	A	W	E

SUITS

P	W	S	C
C	S	W	P
W	C	P	S
S	P	C	W

SUITS

W	S	C	P
C	P	S	W
S	W	P	C
P	C	W	S

FIND THE DIFFERENCE ANSWERS

21 DIFFERENCES HIGHLIGHTED IN BLACK

18 DIFFERENCES HIGHLIGHTED IN BLACK

14 DIFFERENCES HIGHLIGHTED IN BLACK

33 DIFFERENCES HIGHLIGHTED IN BLACK

20 DIFFERENCES HIGHLIGHTED IN BLACK

FIND THE DIFFERENCE ANSWERS

11 DIFFERENCES
HIGHLIGHTED IN BLACK

18 DIFFERENCES
HIGHLIGHTED IN BLACK

HIDDEN OBJECTS ANSWERS

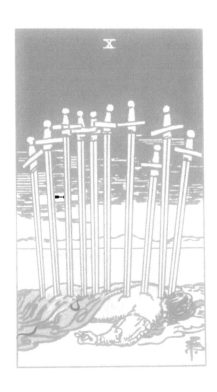

CRYPTOGRAM ANSWERS

A prosperous new beginning. Say "Yes!" to abundance, blessings and luck.

--Ace of Pentacles

You are balancing your obligations well. Focus on priorities.

--Two of Pentacles

Teamwork over the individual. Make sure your partners are equals.

--Three of Pentacles

Security doesn't always come from the material world. Loosen your grip.

--Four of Pentacles

If you take a look around, you can find help. Don't focus on what you are lacking.

--Five of Pentacles

Don't be afraid to be generous with all you have. Giving has its own rewards.

--Six of Pentacles

Plant roots down for the future. Remain patient to reap the benefits of your work later.

--Seven of Pentacles

Find your calling. Hone your path and don't give up.

--Eight of Pentacles

You've reached fulfillment and it feels luxurious. Enjoy the fruits of your labor.

--Nine of Pentacles

You have arrived. You are surrounded by abundance. Share with those you love.

--Ten of Pentacles

A message of stability and prosperity. Are you considering a new path?

--Page of Pentacles

Slow and steady wins the race. It's a long game that cannot be rushed.

--Knight of Pentacles

You can do it all: work, family, independence, abundance and security. Focus on balance.

--Queen of Pentacles

You have created a rich, full life through hard work and responsibility. It's working for you.

--King of Pentacles

A new beginning or idea is being presented. Trust your intuition to guide you forward.

--Ace of Swords

Decisions need to be made. Don't be paralyzed by indecision. Trust your gut.

--Two of Swords

CRYPTOGRAM ANSWERS

Brace yourself for change through pain or truths. Accept in order to heal

--Three of Swords

Give your thoughts a rest. Stepback and recharge your energy in order to heal.

--Four of Swords

Walk away if you need to. Pick your battles and reflect on any power struggles around you.

--Five of Swords

Keep moving ahead. The worst is behind you. Make peace with the past and trust the future.

--Six of Swords

Someone is being sneaky or deceptive. Are you ignoring the signs?

--Seven of Swords

Feeling trapped? You are not stuck. You might be in your own way.

--Eight of Swords

Worry or anxiety is keeping you up at night. Find a way to channel it.

--Nine of Swords

Game over. Stay down, accept the result and reflect on the lessons learned.

--Ten of Swords

Fresh new ideas and a new perspective. Listen to what surrounds you right now.

--Page of Swords

It's time to act! You cannot avoid it. Deal with your situation.

--Knight of Swords

Speak your truth. Communicate clearly and leave emotions out of it.

--Queen of Swords

You didn't get this far by sitting around. Use your communication skills and logic to lead and clear up confusion.

--King of Swords

Love, love, love. New beginnings of positive emotional energy are being presented.

--Ace of Cups

A balancing act of trust, compassion, and respect is needed in any partnership

--Two of Cups

You have found your tribe. Connect and have fun. Be playful and celebrate!

--Three of Cups

Bored and tired of the same old game. Take a look around for the opportunities you are missing.

--Four of Cups

CRYPTOGRAM ANSWERS

Whether it's regret, sorrow, loss or pain, feel it and accept to move on.

--Five of Cups

Reconnect to childlike wonder, playfulness, and a carefree attitude. Have some fun!

--Six of Cups

Consider your many options. Use intuition to focus on one. Stop wishing and start trying.

--Seven of Cups

You don't have to settle. Release the unnecessary in order to move on.

--Eight of Cups

Be satisfied and grateful with your rewards. You've worked hard. Savor it.

--Nine of Cups

You've reached true emotional fulfillment. What's next?

--Ten of Cups

There are messages from unexpected sources or from your own intuition

--Page of Cups

The romantic. Be open to exploring the beautiful ideas in your head and follow your passion.

--Knight of Cups

You are strong. Lead with your heart, trust your intuition and pay attention to your feelings and emotions.

--Queen of Cups

The leader with a big heart. You can use logic and goal setting while making sure others are taken care of.

--King of Cups

Drive and motivation for a new beginning are being offered to help you move.

--Ace of Wands

The future holds possibilities. Make the choice to make your move.

--Two of Wands

You've prepared. Now step outside of your comfort zone and broaden your horizon.

--Three of Wands

Milestones have been met. Celebrate and enjoy the moment before moving on.

--Four of Wands

What are we arguing about? Is something in your way or competing with you?

--Five of Wands

Hard work has paid off. Enjoy the well-deserved victory and recognition. Revel in it.

--Six of Wands

CRYPTOGRAM ANSWERS

Find your ground, take a stand and don't turn your back. Time to be assertive and strategic.

--Seven of Wands

Move fast. It's time for action. There are many choices to move forward but they may not last long.

--Eight of Wands

It's the last stand and you've come a long way. The end is almost in sight.

--Nine of Wands

It's a heavy load. Do you need help with everything you're carrying? The journey is almost over.

--Ten of Wands

You are not short on curiosity, inspiration, or ways to express yourself. Map a strategy.

--Page of Wands

Were you waiting for the green light to bring your new idea to fruition? Start now!

--Knight of Wands

Your confidence shows. You embody creativity, emotional intelligence, and heart-centered actions.

--Queen of Wands

A natural born leader and creative visionary, you are ready to take charge and direct others.

--King of Wands

MATCHING ANSWERS

FIRE: WANDS

WATER: CUPS

AIR: SWORDS

EARTH: PENTACLES

INTELLECT: SWORDS

WEALTH: PENTACLES

PASSION: WANDS

LOVE: CUPS

REASON: SWORDS

DESIRE: WANDS

CAREER: PENTACLES

EMOTION: CUPS

ACTION: WANDS

CLARITY: SWORDS

GROUNDING: PENTACLES

FEELINGS: CUPS

Made in the USA
Thornton, CO
06/14/24 22:35:21